GEORGE LUCAS

GEORGE LUCAS

THE CREATIVE IMPULSE

by Charles Champlin

LUCASFILM'S FIRST TWENTY-FIVE YEARS

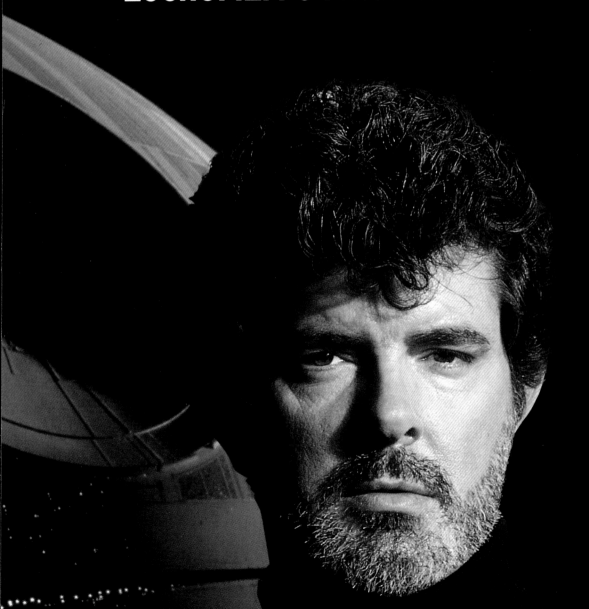

Editor's note

All of George Lucas's principal works have been productions or coproductions of Lucasfilm Ltd. But, in addition, Lucas has used his influence to help other filmmakers he admires get their films financed and distributed. In many cases, he has also lent his guidance to the shaping of the films, with—and sometimes without—formal credit as executive producer. This book looks at those films, as well as Lucas's own major creations, in the order in which they were released.

First published in Great Britain in 1992 by Virgin Books
an imprint of Virgin Publishing Ltd
332 Ladbroke Grove, London, W10 5AH

Reprinted 1994
Revised and updated 1997

First published in 1992 and revised and updated in 1997
by Harry N. Abrams, Inc., New York

A catalogue record for this book is available from the British Library

ISBN 1 85227 721 1

Editor, first edition: Mark Greenberg
Designer: Dana Sloan
Editors for revised and updated edition: Eric Himmel, Rachel Tsutsumi

Printed and bound in Hong Kong

Page 1: Checking out a dolly shot on *THX 1138*, Lucas (center) crouches beside the mobile camera.
Pages 2–3: Photoshop composite by John Knoll
Right: Creating his first feature, George Lucas walks his actors through a scene for *THX 1138*. From the start, beard and gym shoes marked the Lucas look.

CONTENTS

FOREWORD

BY STEVEN SPIELBERG

George Lucas has the best toys of anybody I have ever known, which is why it's so much fun playing over at George's house.

I should have surmised this when we first met at a student-film festival in 1967 where the short film "THX 1138" was not yet a license plate in *American Graffiti* or a state-of-the-art sound system in a couple thousand movie theaters worldwide, but instead a vision of the future of mankind—dark and pessimistic, but nonetheless brilliantly crafted. I was jealous to the very marrow of my bones. I was eighteen years old and had directed fifteen short films by that time, and this little movie was better than all of my little movies combined. No longer were John Ford, Walt Disney, Frank Capra, Federico Fellini, David Lean, Alfred Hitchcock, or Michael Curtiz my role models. Rather, it was someone nearer my own age, someone I could actually get to know, compete with, draw inspiration from.

And twenty-three years later, I'm still drawing incentive from him. Twenty-three years later, George is still doing it better than I. And he's not even directing anymore! He doesn't have to. Because like those of "Uncle" Walt Disney, George's visions burst forth like a galaxy. Like Disney, he has that rare talent of being able to get the best from the people he works with. I know. He got nearly the best out of me in 1981 when I made *Raiders of the Lost Ark*. It was the first time we had actually done the movie business together, and I was determined not to let that get in the way of our fourteen-year-old friendship. So I checked my ego at the door and entered George's world, George's dreams, and I did my utmost to live up to his expectations. The lessons George taught me lasted throughout the 80s. "Don't try to make the greatest movie in the world," he advised during *Raiders* preproduction. "Just get the story told one chapter at a time. Think of this as a B movie." My last three features: *1941, Close Encounters of the Third Kind*, and *Jaws*, each had taken over 130 days to shoot. George gave me 85 days for *Raiders*—a considerably bigger production than *Close Encounters* or *Jaws*—so with an ear always bent in George's direction, I figured I'd finally best him in one way at least. I shot *Raiders* in 73 days, lean and mean, very few outtakes on the cutting room floor. I just told the story.

I've been watching George inspire others ever since. He has built an extraordinary complex in northern California, from where he continues to stretch the limitations of education and entertainment. In fact, the two have often been joined. Three of Lucasfilm's divisions remind me of the innovations and standards they have set. THX says "The Audience is Listening," and today they are listening with greater attention and perception than ever before. Industrial Light and Magic has taken special effects to new heights, making possible what once might not have been imaginable. LucasArts Learning is the latest proof that the breakthroughs in technology developed for the entertainment and business industries can be translated into advances and innovations in education.

Lucasfilm touches our lives from many different directions, descending upon our eyes, our ears, and our children. George has never stopped asking, "Any ideas?" and the whole world has been a better place for it. For two decades I've tried to figure out George's genius. I have tried to unearth it as though it were some archaeological antiquity—George Lucas's crystal ball. After much thought, the only explanation I can offer is this: one day, in a brilliant flash of white light, he saw the future, and he has spent the last twenty years showing it to us.

FOREWORD

BY FRANCIS COPPOLA

It was 1968. I was in a dream world: directing *Finian's Rainbow* on the Warner Brothers lot. Only a few years before I had been a drama student fantasizing about being a film director, and now it was coming true. I was one of the youngest persons on the set, and I was the director. But being a real Hollywood director was a lot different from what I was used to at the UCLA Film School. The happy tradition of sitting around talking about what we would do, of hand-held cameras and cinema verité, of going "on the road" with a small crew, great actors doing scenes about "real" things, was all in the past. Now it was the big time, but with it came the big-time way of doing things: unions, budget and over budget, behind schedule, stunt men, greensmen. Sometimes I felt lonely. Then one day, I saw a skinny young man dressed in a college sweater watching me as I worked on the set. Someone told me he was a student observer from USC. "See anything interesting?" I asked. Slowly he shook his head, and waved his hand, palm down. "Nope, not yet." This is how I met George Lucas.

He had won an award that paid him to be a student observer on the Warners lot. He was on his way to observe the animation department, where he felt the most interesting action was going on. But he had heard of a former UCLA student directing a musical and came over to see what was worthwhile. He stayed on that afternoon, came back the next morning, and became my constant companion and good friend throughout the shooting of the film. During those days, we talked and dreamed about movies and making movies, of going on the road and working with a small crew without the restrictions and prescribed formula for doing everything that was being done every day on the set. We could do it; I could put together a little money, and after *Finian* was over we could work on a film the way the "auteurs" worked. He could write the script he was thinking of, and next he could direct a film as well.

As usual with George, everything we imagined came true. Soon we were on the road shooting *The Rain People.* I was doing a little of my own shooting, and George was bundled up with a Nagra around his neck, doing the sound. Soon that film was over, and driving back to California, we passed through the Napa Valley to San Francisco and had dinner there. We realized we had just made a movie totally on the road; we could be based wherever we wanted to be. Now we could take the entire unit and just plop it down in San Francisco and be independent. George liked the idea. He was from Modesto and had always liked San Francisco.

I went to Germany, to Kohn at the Fotokino, buying editing machines and cameras with money I didn't have. On that trip I visited a company I had heard of called Lanterna Film in Copenhagen. I was thrilled to see a beautiful old mansion with gardens and trees that had been turned into a film company. The many bedrooms had been transformed into editing rooms; the garage was a mixing studio; everywhere young people were working on their films, discussing their projects while eating lunch in the garden.

I came back with these stories, and George and I fantasized about such a company, based in a beautiful place where people could work together while they enjoyed their lives and provided inspiration and advice for one another. We called this film company American Zoetrope and, because no one would sell us an old mansion, started it in a facility we designed ourselves, in the San Francisco industrial neighborhood of South of Market Street. It was a far cry from the pastoral image we had both imagined.

We worked together for a number of years, through *THX 1138, The Godfather, American Graffiti, The Conversation,* and *Apocalypse Now. American Graffiti* gave George the success and money he needed to found Lucasfilm, and he immediately set out to bring the vision we shared into reality—the way he saw it.

Lucasfilm was born, and prospered. It created the Skywalker Ranch, delved into new technology, created classics and sons of classics. And like a twin world born out of the same dream, it remains American Zoetrope's younger and dazzling brother.

Celebrating his fiftieth birthday at Skywalker Ranch, George Lucas is flanked by famous pals: Ron Howard, Steven Spielberg, Martin Scorsese, Brian De Palma, Robert Zemeckis, and Francis Coppola.

When the first edition of *George Lucas: The Creative Impulse* was published in 1992, it seemed fair to say that Lucas—although he was then already twenty years into his career as a filmmaker—had only reached the end of the beginning; there were surely many more achievements to come. Now, five years later, it is obvious that that was a large understatement.

The creative enterprise that Lucas began to build after the success of *American Graffiti* and that is centered on his unique Skywalker Ranch in the hills north of San Francisco has grown so dramatically in both size and diversity that a new edition of this book seemed called for.

This second edition contains twenty-four additional pages of photographs and text, including a section on the newly augmented versions of the original *Star Wars* trilogy released early in 1997. To make the book a more complete reference guide to the work of the various Lucas companies, there are up-to-date lists of their productions and their honors. The inevitable corrections and clarifications have been made in the original text. "I never think of anything as completely finished," Lucas says; "I keep noodling with it."

Central to the excitements of the years since the first appearance of the book has been the extraordinary and continuing affection for *Star Wars* and everything related to the films and their indelible characters. A study by Exhibitor Relations reveals that *Star Wars* stands second only to *Gone With the Wind* in domestic box-office business, expressed in 1996 dollars, and that *The Empire Strikes Back* and *Return of the Jedi* are also among the top twenty all-time box-office successes.

Although there had been no significant theatrical release of the trilogy since *Return of the Jedi* in 1983, *Star Wars*–themed books and merchandise have continued to sell worldwide at phenomenal rates. The adventures in a galaxy far, far away have become classics. Years later, letters regularly arrive at Skywalker Ranch telling how the films have changed the lives of those who saw them, instilling new optimism, courage, and confidence.

Star Wars toys were the fastest-selling items during the 1995–96 Christmas season, and some 30 million units of the *Star Wars* cassettes were sold here and abroad. The further *Star Wars* adventures, nearly two dozen books by various authors, have all been best-sellers. "Nonfiction" books, thoughtful compendiums on *Star Wars* spacecraft and other technologies and the *Star Wars* universe, have also become best-sellers.

LucasArts Entertainment Company has become a major force in computer games, and is now estimated to rank second in the world in sales. Its *Rebel Assault* is one of the most successful titles in personal computer game history, selling more than 1.5 million copies.

The most dynamic development in the Lucas story has been the vindication of George Lucas's long-standing belief (and multimillion-dollar investment) in digital technology as the wave of the future for filmmaking.

Having revolutionized visual effects with their work on the *Star Wars* trilogy, Lucas and his Industrial Light & Magic have now wrought a second revolution with the astonishing computer graphics made possible by digital technology. ILM has contributed to more than a hundred films, including *Twister, Jurassic Park, Jumanji,* and *Casper* (the friendly ghost who was entirely a creation of computer graphics), and has had a part in six of the ten largest-grossing films of all time. In the last seventeen years, it has won fourteen Academy Awards for Best Achievement in Visual Effects.

The release of the *Star Wars Trilogy Special Edition*—each film now reedited and enhanced to reflect fully the creative intentions Lucas had for them but could not entirely fulfill because of shortages of time, money, or technology—was memorably nostalgic for millions, a dazzling first-time experience for newer generations.

Since the original appearance of this book, Lucas has restructured the organization into three major companies—Lucasfilm Ltd., Lucas Digital Ltd. (Industrial Light & Magic and Skywalker Sound), and LucasArts Entertainment Company (interactive entertainment). The components, like ILM and Games, which he once referred to as "his children," now ready to be on their own and become self-sustaining profit centers, have succeeded beyond anybody's dreams.

The new corporate structure, with each company largely self-governing, has enabled Lucas to divorce himself from the pressure of daily details and innumerable meetings, to let his imagination run free of distraction.

In recent months, he has been coming into his Skywalker Ranch office only one day a week. He is otherwise holed up in a small studio at his home, where he has been working on the scripts of the first installments of the next trilogy, which will actually be the originating episodes of the whole *Star Wars* epic, begun in 1977 with Episode Four. He is doing extended treatments of the next two episodes, overseeing preproduction planning on all three episodes, and plotting as well a possible fourth Indiana Jones adventure for Steven Spielberg and Harrison Ford.

The new *Star Wars* trilogy will involve not only the new wonders of digital technology but the lessons Lucas and his production team learned about nonlinear filmmaking during the three-year making of "The Young Indiana Jones Chronicles." Lucas himself will direct the first movie in the new trilogy—the last film he directed was *Star Wars* more than twenty years ago. The film is expected to be released in 1999. If it succeeds (Lucas is modest enough to raise the question), the second and third films will, he says, probably be made simultaneously, directed by others.

Then, he says, he may be able to take it a little easier.

It is possible, of course, that George Lucas can indeed take it easier, but based on past performance it is unlikely that he will. Digital technology continues to evolve, and Lucas is determined that ILM will stay in the forefront. Already, through fiber-optic cable, ILM can collaborate on computer graphics with producers at screens almost anywhere in the world. Ultimately Lucas envisions that the whole postproduction process will be fully digitalized, at enormous gains in quality and reductions in time and cost.

In yet another ramification of the digital revolution, Lucas is determined to push the educational potential of multimedia interactivity: the CD-ROM linked to the personal computer, and ultimately involving networked interactivity as well. He recently formed Lucas Learning to commence developing educational interactive products for home consumption. As the necessary technology becomes available, Lucas also plans to convert "The Young Indiana Jones Chronicles," soon to be available as full-length movies on video, into interactive learning products. Several years ago he formed his George Lucas Educational Foundation to support research into ways of improving educational methods, especially as they involve interactive technology.

"The interactive version of the 'Chronicles' is ten years ahead of its time," Lucas says. "The technology will have to catch up." Then again, he adds, "I'm always looking way, way forward; that's where the excitement is."

If Lucas, hardly into his fifties, is beyond the end of the beginning, it is possible to say that he is perhaps in the middle of the middle, continuing to be a soft-voiced revolutionary who does not so much find worlds to conquer as he does invent them.

INTRODUCTION

Lucas Valley Road runs west from the freeway, US 101, in Marin County a few miles north of the Golden Gate Bridge. It's a two-lane blacktop that grows thinner after it passes an upmarket housing development. Thereafter, the road meanders through rolling hills, dipping and twisting, rising and falling, passing stands of live oak and evergreens, an occasional farm building, and the occasional cow grazing on the slopes. Young deer come to the road's edge to stare fearlessly at the few passing cars. The existence of the San Francisco metropolis and the bedroom communities of Marin—the whole hustle of the modern commercial world—seems to recede with every bend in the road.

Eight miles in, there's an easy-to-miss turnoff, marked by a low and unobtrusive sign and by a pair of electronic gates. A narrow road leads beyond the gates, but there's nothing else to be seen except gentle fields rising toward substantial hills in the distance.

This is the entrance to George Lucas's Skywalker Ranch, a filmmaker's unprecedented investment in the future of filmmaking and in the act of creativity. Hidden in the folds of the hills are several buildings. One, which resembles a turn-of-the-century winery, with a small vineyard before it, houses one of the best postproduction facilities in the motion-picture industry, including a state-of-the-art recording stage used by artists as various as Linda Ronstadt, the Kronos Quartet, and the Grateful Dead. Well up the road, past a man-made lake constructed as a home for migratory birds and as a source of water for fire prevention, is a cluster of buildings that flank a large white house designed in the Victorian style, with fine verandas and a solarium.

The main house is the headquarters of George Lucas, who designed it as he designed all the other structures on the Ranch. (The road itself is named not for George but for a much earlier landowner of the same name. The coincidence suggests that fate has been at work.)

The whole complex covers some 2,700 acres, of which no more than 5 percent can ever be developed, the remaining 95 percent deeded to a permanent preserve through the Marin Agricultural Land Trust. The complex constitutes what might be called a "think-ranch," an oasis for creativity, conceived by Lucas and dedicated to the proposition that men and women can be more creative, more ingenious, more imaginative when they are comfortable, congenial, and—insofar as it is possible in the twentieth century—unstressed and undistracted by the pressures and exasperations of daily life.

It is, in a real sense, the dream that *American Graffiti* built, as well as *Star Wars* and *The Empire Strikes Back* and *Return of the Jedi* and the Indiana Jones trilogy, commencing with *Raiders of the Lost Ark*, which Lucas created for his friend and frequent collaborator Steven Spielberg.

Already a major figure in American filmmaking after *American Graffiti* and *Star Wars*, Lucas at 38 still looked collegiate in jeans and sneakers as, bandanna'ed against the blowing sands of a Tunisian desert, he oversaw a scene from *Return of the Jedi*.

Lucas as a moppet in Modesto (top) enjoyed a boyhood he remembers as more Midwestern than Californian.

Smiling for his class photo at Downey High School, Lucas thought that writing and anthropology rather than filmmaking were likely to be his future. He was also studying history and philosophy.

At USC, Lucas discovered that in fact he had a natural gift for filmmaking and was soon (right) hard at it.

As George Lucas completed his first twenty years as a filmmaker, he and Spielberg had between them created what stood as eight of the ten most popular films released to that date: the two trilogies (*Star Wars* and Indiana Jones) plus Spielberg's *ET* and *Jaws*. By now, the *Star Wars* films have taken in something more than a billion dollars at U.S. box offices alone. Merchandise themed to the *Star Wars* characters, from T-shirts to lunch pails to comics and other books, has accounted for more than $2 billion in retail sales worldwide, and almost two decades after *Star Wars* first appeared, it continues to sell.

Star Wars was a phenomenon, and not only in its unprecedented success at the box office. It launched a revolution in the science of motion-picture special effects, using computer-controlled cameras and other advanced techniques to create fantasy on a scale and with a believability that the movies had never known before. The revolution is still in progress, and in its front rank is Industrial Light and Magic, the special-effects firm that Lucas founded in 1975 and that is now located in lively and crowded quarters not far from the Ranch in San Rafael, California. By now, ILM services not only Lucas's own films but the whole industry, contributing to films like *The Abyss, Back to the Future II,* and *Ghost.*

There is a sequence ILM did for *Terminator II* in which a puddle of liquid on a floor takes shape and rises in the form of the metal-clad Terminator, which then evolves into an ordinary workman (and an identifiable human actor). It boggles the mind.

Then again, George Lucas has been boggling the mind ever since he was a student filmmaker at the University of Southern California. One of his student films, a suspenseful fantasy about a fascistic society in some not-too-far-off tomorrow, "THX 1138:4EB (Electronic Labyrinth)," was such an imaginative tour de force (using parking structures to suggest the brutal gray prison-like world of tomorrow) that it led to his first commercial feature.

As a close friend of his has observed, Lucas has emerged as part Walt Disney, part Thomas A. Edison, part Henry David Thoreau, and in his financial shrewdness, part A. P. Giannini (the founder of the Bank of America). This was said tongue in cheek. Yet the links to Disney and Edison are obvious. His independence is almost legendary. And, unique among filmmakers of this or any other time, Lucas is an astute businessman, a fiscal conservative who does not mind taking huge financial risks, so sure is he of his judgments.

His foresight in obtaining and retaining the merchandising rights to his films, and the rights to the sequels of his films, has hugely

An avid car enthusiast, as a teenager Lucas made money photographing racing cars and drivers. In 1988 he was still driving his C-sports racer.

increased his earnings and helped make possible the enormous investment he has made in the Ranch, at ILM, and in a new postproduction facility in Santa Monica, California.

Like Edison (who was also a tough businessman), Lucas is an innovator who takes particular delight in tackling problems (as in special effects) that appear to be insoluble but that, in the end, are solved, often by finding new ways of doing things.

Lucas has read deeply in mythology and anthropology and is a great admirer of the writings of Joseph Campbell, whose views on the myths by which we live are reflected in Lucas's work, notably the *Star Wars* trilogy and *Willow*. It was no accident that television journalist Bill Moyers's in-depth interviews with Campbell were taped at Skywalker Ranch.

Like Thoreau, Lucas is at heart a maverick who cherishes his independence and, to preserve it, has turned his back on Hollywood. As a product of northern California, Lucas was never comfortable in Los Angeles, while he was a USC student, graduating in 1966, or as a young learner, working for and with Francis Coppola at Warner Brothers. Lucas returned to northern California as quickly as he could, in 1969, and since then he has, in effect, persuaded Hollywood (that is, the industry) to come to him.

What remains unique about Lucas in an industry where the rule is to take the money and run is that he has poured millions back into it. Only his friend Francis Coppola has tried to do anything on a comparable scale, and while his brave effort at creating a studio in Hollywood could not be sustained, Coppola's Zoetrope continues to function in San Francisco. And it was the vision of a filmmakers' commune, which Coppola and Lucas had discussed during the filming of *The Rain People* in the idealistic 60s—a place where they could make their films the way they wanted to make them, outside the pressures and constraints of Hollywood—that led to Skywalker Ranch.

Having made his reputation and the beginnings of his fortune as the writer and director of *American Graffiti* and *Star Wars,* Lucas has, in subsequent years, preferred to concentrate on his role as producer, which includes the generating of story ideas, as for the Indy pictures and several others. That way, Lucas has said, he can keep several irons in the fire at once. The projects these days include not only films and an ambitious television series but, most especially, experiments with interactive multimedia productions as a teaching tool. Not least among the elements in Lucas's makeup is a strong strain of social idealism. One of the functions he envisions for Skywalker Ranch is as a venue for great minds and futurist thinkers to gather together and plot better days for a world that could sorely use them.

As the chief executive of the multimillion-dollar enterprise that Lucasfilm Ltd. came to be almost overnight, Lucas has had to endure some painful corporate convulsions as the company sought to find its stride, its proper size, and the right management team. In more recent times, he has been moving to divorce himself from the day-to-day pressures of corporate life.

The various divisions, including ILM and Skywalker Sound, have been collected under a new corporate umbrella called LucasArts Entertainment Company. They have now been designated as profit centers, soon to be, if not presently, self-sustaining. "I think of them as my children," Lucas said with a grin not long ago. "I've raised them, and now they're on their own and off to college."

Lucasfilm Ltd. is now Lucas himself and a relatively small number of close coworkers who will help Lucas concentrate on a limited number of personal projects—television series and films that he will produce and possibly direct. He is under persuasive pressure from fans to do a new *Star Wars* trilogy, probably a prequel to the existing trilogy.

As it is, Lucasfilm is just into its third decade, not yet a quarter-century old. But as the photographs in this book forcefully remind us, George Lucas's impact on the imagination everywhere on earth and his influence within the world of filmmaking have been extraordinary. The two trilogies are central ornaments in the history of film—prime examples of the movies at their storytelling, engrossing best. Still other films on which Lucas has been cocreator, executive producer, collaborator, urger, and encourager have made their own ways into film history.

The industry's admiration for all that Lucas has wrought was most tellingly expressed early in 1992 when the governors of the Academy of Motion Picture Arts and Sciences voted him its highest, rarest, most coveted honor, the Irving G. Thalberg Award. Previous recipients, legendary names in Hollywood, have included Darryl F. Zanuck, Alfred Hitchcock, Walt Disney, and Steven Spielberg. Despite the achievements of his first two decades, what seems clear is that George Lucas has only reached the end of the beginning.

In 1977, with *Star Wars* an authentic hit, R2-D2 and C-3PO arrived to leave their metallic footprints in cement in the famous forecourt at Mann's Chinese Theater on Hollywood Boulevard, drawing a crowd of several thousand fans.

George Lucas was born in Modesto, California, a fast-growing farm center at the northern end of the San Joaquin Valley, in 1944. His boyhood—putting on circuses and carnivals in the backyard, building Soap Box Derby racers in a park not far from the house—would have been appropriate to an Andy Hardy movie. "Even though it's California, it was a quiet Midwestern kind of upbringing. There wasn't much going on," Lucas says.

His father owned a stationery store and sold office supplies and equipment. George helped out, unpacking and shelving the stock. He has two older sisters and a younger one. His mother was a frequent invalid while he was growing up, and he was largely tended by his sisters and a housekeeper. He had been fanatically interested in cars from childhood, so sixteen became a magic age for him. He could drive legally, he became the store's delivery boy, and he acquired the first car of his own. "It was a very small Fiat, which I souped up," he says.

He helped out in a Renault garage, where he could work on his car after hours. "Then at night I'd cruise the main street, with all the other guys in their cars." He also raced in autocrosses—cars competing against the clock. It was, of course, the life-style of these growing-up years in the 50s that Lucas recaptured so exceptionally well in *American Graffiti,* which was his first commercial success and the film that established his reputation both as an innovative filmmaker and as a man who knew where the audience was and how to capture its attention and hold its loyalty.

Then, driving on a quiet rural road a few days before he was due to graduate from high school, Lucas was in a near-fatal automobile accident, in circumstances not unlike the wreck in which James Dean had died a few years earlier. Lucas narrowly survived, but with crushed lungs, which required a long and life-changing convalescence. It became clear to him that life did not stretch on endlessly and that you had best make full use of the years granted to you.

He went to Modesto Junior College for two years. Having been bored silly in high school, and with grades to prove it, he now began to read voraciously in psychology and anthropology, and he took creative-writing courses. The grades improved dramatically. He was accepted at San Francisco State as an English major, intending to pursue his possibilities as a writer. But a childhood pal persuaded him to take the entrance exams for USC. The USC cinema school, the pal said, would let Lucas follow his interests in writing as well as in photography, which he had begun to practice professionally around his car-racing friends. To his pleased amazement, Lucas was accepted.

Still at USC, Lucas was invited to film a documentary on the making of *Mackenna's Gold,* produced by Carl Foreman (left) and starring Gregory Peck. "6.18.67" had little to do with the film but won prizes.

Working on a student film "1:42:08" in 1966, Lucas (not yet beard-bearing) directed a cameraman mounted horizontally beside a race car.

"I realized that I'd found myself," Lucas says. "I loved working with film, and I was pretty good at it. So I took the bit and ran with it. I was introduced to film editing—the whole concept of editing—and I think ultimately that film editing was where my real talent was. Still is, I guess."

When Lucas finished his undergraduate work, he took jobs as an editor, grip, and second-unit cameraman. That fall he was given a chance to be a teaching assistant in the cinema school's camera department, giving a special course to a class of Marine and Navy cameramen. He seized it as a chance to work on a project he had been developing called "THX 1138:4EB." "To have this young hippie come in and teach them after they'd been at it for ten years was a challenge. But the whole idea of the class was to teach them they didn't have to go by the rule book."

He divided the class in half, each half to make a film. The men working directly with Lucas shot "THX 1138:4EB." It was an exercise in using available light, with only three small floods for occasional filling in. Whatever his students learned from the experience, it was a significant move for Lucas.

Lucas decided to stay at USC for a master's degree. He continued to edit "THX" and worked on additional films, his own and those of his classmates. He made a documentary, "The Emperor," about a Los Angeles disc jockey who called himself Emperor Hudson, and other short films called "Herbie," "1.42.08," and "Anyone Lived in a Pretty How Town." He did the editing and sound recording on a wicked animated satire of the films of Michelangelo Antonioni called "Marcello, I'm So Bored" by John Milius.

Then Lucas entered his work in the National Student Film Festival and won prizes in every category. "THX" took top prize in the drama category. "The Emperor" won honorable mention in the documentary category and another, called "6.18.67," got honorable mention in the experimental category. The triple play confirmed that Lucas was more than ever a young man to watch.

"THX," in particular, remains a subtle and sophisticated piece of filmmaking—dark, moody, foreboding, a look into an oppressive future, with eerie sound effects like voices on a bad connection or over the public-address system in a European train station. It is a film intended to be felt as much as understood, and it was to be his ticket to the commercial film world.

In the summer of 1967 Lucas was chosen as one of four student filmmakers (two each from USC and UCLA) to create short

In the summer of 1964 he moved to Los Angeles and bunked in with two friends in a pad in Malibu, paying his share of the rent by selling his paintings of surfer girls with eyes as wide and wistful as those of the artist Keane's kitschy children. Lucas met the cinematographer Haskell Wexler, who was to become a close friend and a visual consultant on *American Graffiti*.

In his first production course, in animation, at the university, Lucas demonstrated that he had found a home, and a destiny, in filmmaking. The instructor, Herb Kossower, gave the students one minute of film stock with which to explore the workings of the camera. Lucas took his 32 feet of film and made a "kinestasis" film, in which still pictures were photographed for a few frames only, so that they seemed to flash on the screen at dazzling speed. Lucas called the short "Look at Life." Kossower entered the one-

films for producer Carl Foreman around the making of *McKenna's Gold,* which J. Lee Thompson was directing. The PBS outlet in Los Angeles did a special about the project, featuring Foreman, the four filmmakers, and their films. Foreman at first opposed Lucas's film, the subsequently honored "6.18.67," on grounds that it had nothing to do with the feature itself. It was a desert tone poem, using camera trickeries to create a rather surrealistic celebration of the desert. It was clearly the most innovative and original of the four films, as Foreman ultimately and privately agreed.

That fall, Lucas won the annual scholarship to serve as an apprentice at Warner Brothers. Jack Warner had just sold the studio to Seven Arts and in the transition period only one film was being shot on the lot: Francis Coppola's adaptation of the musical *Finian's Rainbow,* starring Fred Astaire and Petula Clark. One of Lucas's USC classmates, Howard Kazanjian, was second assistant director on the film. Lucas hung out with him and soon met Coppola himself, who was to be an important figure in his career.

Coppola started giving Lucas jobs to do on the set, and he eventually became Coppola's assistant. When *Finian's Rainbow* was completed, Coppola talked Warners into giving Lucas a contract to turn "THX" into a feature script. The money enabled Lucas to join Coppola's small crew (twelve) on the cross-country shooting of *The Rain People,* which featured James Caan as a brain-damaged football player.

On the road, Lucas says, "I'd get up at four in the morning and write on *THX* until it was time to go to work for Francis at seven. By the time we were finished looking at dailies, it was always ten or eleven at night, but I was young and it was fun." He worked as an assistant to almost everyone on the crew: cameraman, sound man, art director. But he also kept a 16mm camera and a Nagra tape recorder with him, capturing Coppola at work. The documentary, called *Filmmaker,* was finished in 1968.

Principal photography on *The Rain People* ended in Ogallala, Nebraska. "Francis kept saying, 'We don't have to make films in Hollywood. We can be anywhere in the world we want to be.'"

By a timely happenstance, Lucas flew to San Francisco to substitute for Coppola at a convention. There he met a young independent filmmaker named John Korty. "That was ironic," Korty said not long ago. "If there's one thing in the world George hates to do, it's speak in public." They both addressed a national gathering of English teachers, and later Korty described his studio, a barn he rented for $100 a month at Stinson Beach just north of San Francisco. There he had made *Funnyman,* which had been shown at the New York Film Festival in 1968.

After an internship at Warners, Lucas joined Francis Coppola's small crew on *The Rain People* and (top) began a documentary on the director at work.

Experienced in most of the filmmaking skills, Lucas helped out on *The Rain People* as occasional sound recordist among other tasks.

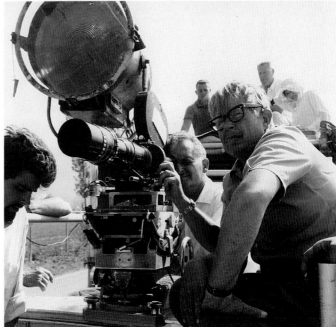

Fred Astaire danced again in *Finian's Rainbow* (opposite), the only film in production at Warners when Lucas arrived for the internship he had won. He found a kindred spirit in Francis Coppola, who was directing.

Coppola (top), a **UCLA** film school graduate, had first won attention as a writer before being given a major Hollywood musical to direct.

Serving his apprenticeship on *Finian's Rainbow,* Lucas kept an observant eye on the script and the work of cinematographer Philip Lathrop (looking into the camera, above) and his operator.

"George went right to a pay phone and called Francis in Nebraska and said, 'You gotta see this,'" Korty remembers. "They came out on the Fourth of July, 1969. They were amazed to see that I had an editing table, everything I needed. Francis said, 'If you can do it, I can do it.'"

Coppola went on an equipment-buying spree in Europe and saw another independent film operation set up in a Copenhagen mansion. Back in the U.S., he and Lucas began looking for a Victorian mansion to buy in Marin County, but the idea proved too expensive and complicated. Meanwhile, the equipment was arriving from Europe. With Korty's help, they found and rented a warehouse in San Francisco. They called the operation American Zoetrope, with Coppola as president and Lucas as vice president. Coppola began postproduction on *The Rain People* while Lucas wrestled with the script for a feature-length version of "THX."

Warners had changed hands again and Coppola talked the new management into funding a series of low-budget films he promised would be in the low-cost but high-profit tradition of *Easy Rider,* whose huge success with critics and audiences had made a deep impression on Hollywood executives. One of the films in production would be Lucas's *THX.*

Film-school friends of both Coppola and Lucas came up to join Zoetrope, including John Milius, who was working with George on a script of what became *Apocalypse Now.* "We were," Lucas says, "a loose confederation of radicals and hippies."

Lucas's deepest interests at that point were photography, animation, and film editing. Combining all those interests, he grew fascinated by the possibilities of a kind of abstract filmmaking: nonlinear, noncharacter, nonstory. He had discovered, he said, "that with a camera and an editing machine, you can move people to tears." In San Francisco, he told himself, he would make avant-garde films and find a living as a cinema-verité documentary filmmaker. What is significant in retrospect is that even the fantasy films like *Star Wars* derive much of their power from the seeming verity of the telling.

But, at the moment, there was what appeared to be a significant opportunity to demonstrate the viability of Zoetrope, while making a very personal film with the backing of a major Hollywood studio.

On a wet day on the road during *The Rain People,* Lucas waited with crew members. Crossing the country by car, the Coppola crew numbered scarcely a dozen.

Sporting a Vandyke toward the end of *The Rain People* days, Lucas felt very much in the radical spirit of the 60s, impatient with traditional filmmaking and eager to experiment.

THX 1138 (1971)

The script for the original, student-film version of "THX 1138:4EB," as it was then known, had begun as a brief idea of Lucas's. He was graduating and tried to convince his pals Matthew Robbins (who later wrote Steven Spielberg's *Sugarland Express*) and Walter Murch to develop it as their final filmmaking project. They did a treatment but did not make the film, so George scripted it and shot it in the cinematography class he was teaching.

Preparing the feature version for Warners, Lucas worked on the script with several hands, but the final version was written by Lucas and Murch, who had come up to San Francisco to do the sound editing for Coppola on *The Rain People*.

Lucas acquired some excellent casting—Robert Duvall, early in his career, as the worker who has accidentally received free will in his incarcerating world of tomorrow; the British veteran Donald Pleasence as the chief villain; Maggie McOmie as the love interest, remarkably beautiful even with her head shaved as required by the script.

The feature, like the short, is essentially one long and very suspenseful pursuit. Lucas showed again his amazing resourcefulness by shooting in subway tunnels and parking structures to convey the blank but hostile concrete surfaces of "the encased city of tomorrow," as one article described it, "an electronic, computerized dictatorship that created its workers to specifications, as little more than automatons with heartbeats." The soundtrack was a nightmarish river of yawps and wheeps, echoing alarms and disembodied voices.

Ted Moehnke, a San Francisco carpenter-prop man hired to work on the film, remembered that to get the look of a tomorrow world, "We shot in and out of all the BART subway tunnels before they were finished, at the Marin County Civic Center [an avant-garde design by Frank Lloyd Wright], and around the Lawrence Livermore atomic-energy laboratory. We drove around in the van Francis Coppola used on *The Rain People,* and my prop cart was a garbage can with wheels."

Lalo Schifrin, a young musician-composer from Buenos Aires just making his own start in Hollywood, did the score for *THX 1138* and remembers that Lucas's first imagination-stretching question was, What would the Muzak of the future be like? "We needed a soporific music that makes everybody kind of slow-witted," Schifrin says. They agreed on the sounds of electronic clarinet, accordion, and organ. "I had to write, if you'll excuse the expression, stupid music, purposely stupid music, which is hard to

THX 1138

Robert Duvall (above) in an early role starred in the feature version of *THX 1138,* playing a man accidentally granted free will in a robotic society.

The future society, with its own big brother, that Lucas envisioned in *THX 1138* had policemen who were the more compassionate because they were robots.

THX 1138

Using real structures as his glimpses of tomorrow, Lucas tried a climbing action as part of Duvall's escape from the imprisoning city (top).

Lucas explains how he wants a scene played to one of the robotic cops with their ghostly makeup.

Before his break for freedom, Duvall (opposite) does his sterile chores in the laboratory where the robots are manufactured.

do—purposely." That was the ambient music. Schifrin also wrote an underscore, austere and oppressive, "creating the anguish of the kind of Orwellian society George had invented."

Coppola flew down to Los Angeles to show the studio the finished film plus several scripts that he and others at Zoetrope had been working on. "Warners hated them all, including the film," Lucas says wryly. "They told Francis we were going to have to pay back all the money they'd advanced. It was a dire time."

("My topsy-turvy finances have always terrified George," Coppola now says with a laugh. "But if I hadn't been borrowing madly at the beginning, we'd never have got things going. He's very conservative. Yet he's one of the very, very few filmmakers who have earned a great fortune in the business and poured it back into the business.")

The studio chopped five minutes out of the film. It received mixed reviews, the atmosphere and the action highly praised, the dialogue and the characterizations found pallid beside the excitements of the chase. But six years later, capitalizing on the huge success of *Star Wars, THX 1138* was re-released (with the five cut minutes edited back in by Lucas). By then it was possible to see that *THX* had been prophetic of Lucas if not yet of the world. His precocious mastery of the medium was evident, and so was the essential warmth of his prevailing view—innocent, imaginative, and, despite all that he found alarming in society, finally optimistic.

"Then we had to go our separate ways," Lucas says. Coppola went off to do *The Godfather* to restore his own financial fortunes, and Lucas formed his own company, called Lucasfilm Ltd.

Lucas had tried to get *Apocalypse Now* off the ground, but he couldn't find a taker. He reluctantly abandoned the project and began to develop the screenplay for what became *American Graffiti.* After turndowns elsewhere, Universal expressed interest. "The buzz was that *Godfather* was going to be a giant hit. So Universal said that, if Francis would put his name on the film, they would give it the go-ahead." Francis would. So, after an uncertain start in the real, postgraduate world of filmmaking, Lucas was ready to do the film that would make his reputation.

THX 1138

The robot cops, wielding their long batons, corner Duvall as he is revealed as a man with feelings. The featureless, characterless walls were part of Lucas's foreboding design for a dismal future.

Duvall's shaven head is calibrated for clues to his aberrant nature (opposite left).

Duvall and Maggie McOmie defy authority and find romance (opposite center).

Maggie McOmie (opposite right), her head shaven as a symbol of her slave status, conveyed the forlorn despair of the nightmarish tomorrow Lucas was depicting.

AMERICAN GRAFFITI (1973)

Nothing in Hollywood happens easily. George Lucas's first feature, *THX 1138,* had attracted some decent reviews but few customers. It was, however, accepted for the prestigious Directors Fortnight program at the Cannes Film Festival. Lucas and his then wife, Marcia, who had moved from Los Angeles back to northern California in 1969, had just $2,000 in the bank. But Lucas fatalistically decided to blow most of it on a visit to Cannes, with some backpacking around Europe to follow.

At the festival, he made a deal with David Picker of United Artists for $10,000 to develop a script for *American Graffiti.* (Lacking a festival pass, he had had to sneak into the screening of his own film.)

Lucas had been shooting some sequences of *THX* at an old studio in Los Angeles when his USC classmate Willard Huyck and Huyck's wife and writing partner, Gloria Katz, paid him a visit. Huyck remembered not long ago that Lucas said, "I have an idea I'd love you guys to do. It's a rock 'n' roll movie and it takes place in the 50s and it's about cruising and music and deejays."

Huyck and Katz and Lucas subsequently roughed out the eight-page treatment that Picker had liked. "To this day, it's still the movie," Huyck says. But by the time Lucas made the deal with UA, Huyck and Katz were off doing a horror film and could not work on the project. Lucas gave another writer the $10,000 to do a script but found it totally unacceptable. By now, the Lucas exchequer was down to $500. "We were practically destitute," Lucas remembers. Yet at the time he was being pressured to direct a film in Florida for $100,000 plus a piece of the profits. He disliked the script, as well as the idea of doing someone else's story, and broke as he was, he turned down the offer. The film, when it was made, turned out to be a disaster. "My career would have been ruined if I'd done it; that would have been the end of me," Lucas says.

Lucas wrote several drafts of *American Graffiti,* which UA rejected. But with the promise of Francis Coppola as producer and advisor, Universal agreed to take a chance on a picture that was described as nothing more than a musical montage. By then Huyck and Katz had finished the horror film and were able to rejoin

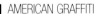

AMERICAN GRAFFITI

A perfect symbol of an earlier and seemingly simpler time, Mel's Drive-In was the focal point of much of the action in *American Graffiti.*

Lucas as coauthors of the final script. For Universal the project was not a major risk: a budget of only $700,000 and a shooting schedule of only twenty-eight days. Most major studio productions have schedules twice that long or longer.

Coppola urged Lucas to have Fred Roos, who had done much of the casting on *Godfather*, help him with the casting of *American Graffiti*. "We decided to make a massive search for good kids, and that's what it was, massive; it went on for weeks and months," Roos says. Roos had cast Ron Howard in television shows and liked him, but there was then still a prejudice about using television performers in feature films. "'People won't pay to see actors they can watch for free,' that was the studio argument," says Roos.

Ron Howard has his own memories of the casting. "I went for a meeting and the man turned out to be unlike any director I'd ever met. He was wearing a school jacket and had a beard. I'd heard it was going to be a musical, and I warned him that I'd been hired for *The Music Man* because I *couldn't* sing. George said, 'Don't worry. You won't have to sing.' We did cold readings, improvisations, video tests, everything. Five interviews and six months later I was cast." It was the start of a long, close association and friendship between Lucas and Howard.

Fred Roos says, "I knew Cindy Williams, Candy Clark, and Ricky—that's what we called him then—Ricky Dreyfuss." He had cast Candy Clark in a small role in John Huston's *Fat City* and had helped Cindy Williams get her first agent and a part in the TV sitcom "Room 222." He had proposed Paul Le Mat as one of the leads in *Fat City*. Charlie Martin Smith came out of the interviewing process, and Roos had seen McKenzie Phillips singing with a teenage band at the Troubadour nightclub in Los Angeles.

"Harrison Ford I knew, too," Roos adds. "He'd done carpentry for me between his acting jobs."

The movie was inspired by Lucas's own teenage years in Modesto, but the city had grown so fast in the postwar years it would no longer work as the location. Instead, Lucas chose San Rafael, near where he was living. Much of the action takes place at night as the teenagers cruise the main drag in their cars. Lucas made a deal to pay $300 a night for permission to shoot on the streets. But after only one night a bar owner complained that the filming was keeping his customers away, and the city withdrew its cooperation. "On the second night I was half a day behind schedule and I'd lost my main set," Lucas remembers. "I was devastated." But a production assistant explored Petaluma, a bit farther north; the town was very cooperative and most of the picture was finally photographed there.

Mackenzie Phillips was a precocious teenager with a massive crush on Paul Le Mat, the aspiring race driver (and another of Lucas's alter egos).

Taking revenge on some girls who teased her, Phillips sprays shaving cream on a windshield and writes an angry message in it (below).

Harrison Ford recalls the whole experience—his first with Lucas—with great amusement. "At the first interview, George was so quiet I didn't know which one he was." Once shooting began, Ford says, "George was under incredible strain. He was working his tail to the bone. It was such a low-cost production that we didn't have a camera car, for example. What we did was haul one picture car with another picture car on a trailer we'd rented from U-Haul. Then we took the trunk lid off the lead car so the sound man, the cameraman, and George could crouch in the trunk.

"I remember a scene where we had to circle the block again and again and again. Afterward, we went up to the camera car to see how it had gone, and George had fallen asleep in the trunk."

At first, the production seemed jinxed, commencing with the loss of San Rafael on the second night of shooting. That same night, the assistant cameraman fell off the makeshift camera car and was run over by the trailer. No bones broken or serious damage, but it represented a loss of precious shooting time, crowned later in the evening when a greater-alarm fire closed down the main street for the rest of the night. "Somehow we finished the film on time, but the troubles didn't bode well."

Lucas turned the finished film over to the studio, which didn't much like it. In the lobby after the first sneak preview, Coppola got into a shouting match with some studio executives, who were talking about cuts and changes, and he demanded he be allowed to buy the film back and take it to another distributor. The studio declined.

"They wanted it shorter," Lucas remembers. "But there was a Writers Guild strike on, and I couldn't go on the lot. So they cut five minutes out of it, and I was furious."

Lucas's revenge was sweet. The reviews were sensational ("One of the most important films of the year, as well as the one most likely to move you to tears"—*Los Angeles Times*). And so was the box office. Made for only $700,000, it brought Universal more than $50 million in rentals, possibly the biggest return on investment in Hollywood's modern history.

Lucas had not simply re-created his own eighteenth summer (1962), he had created a then-unique narrative style in which several different and unrelated stories intertwine. Subsequently, the technique has become almost standard in hour-long television series like "L. A. Law" and "Hill Street Blues." The film's use of a musical collage to underscore the action and reinforce the feeling of the period was also then unique. There were forty-one songs by thirty-five groups on the track, with Bill Haley and the Comets, the Regents, and Buddy Holly among them, and with Flash Cadillac

AMERICAN GRAFFITI

The roller-skating carhops (above) at Mel's Drive-In were already an endangered species and are now virtually extinct in America.

Hunched beneath the counter at the diner (opposite), Lucas directs a love-sad Ron Howard as cinematographer Haskell Wexler watches the image.

AMERICAN GRAFFITI

Paul Le Mat's hoodless and souped-up yellow roadster, a blur of motion, was the perfect embodiment of Lucas's own passionate love of cars and speed as a teenager in Modesto.

Han Solo and Indiana Jones still in his future, Harrison Ford had a supporting role as a post–high-school hot-rodder with the fastest car in town.

In his movie debut, Le Mat made a strong impression as the moody loner with a fierce ambition to go fast (above).

and the Continental Kids on camera. Disc jockey Wolfman Jack was a kind of hoarse-voiced deity, sending his siren songs and his personalized chat into the California night.

The night shooting, which would have been impossible technologically only a few years before, was also an innovation. There were, in fact, problems the first couple of nights. Then Lucas's early Los Angeles friend, the cinematographer Haskell Wexler, who was shooting commercials during the day, flew up every night and served as supervising cameraman and visual consultant on the film, solving the difficult problems posed by the night shooting on a limited budget and time schedule.

American Graffiti was, not least, further proof that a new generation of filmmakers was emerging from the nation's campuses. Coppola's *The Godfather* had been released in March 1972, a year and a half before *Graffiti* appeared in August 1973. Lucas's film was unique in that it was the first time the new generation had looked to its own experience.

The age of John F. Kennedy had begun and ended as the Lucas generation was growing up, and JFK is a kind of off-camera presence in *American Graffiti.* There is latent violence in the film, and danger, sadness, true romance, and a good deal of stirring in the loins; yet the tone of the film is wonderful innocence.

Lucas's nostalgic affection was combined with a cool detachment that saw the last days of high school as the last days of a special confidence as well (only slightly shadowed by anxiety) before the mature world with all its disappointments and its limitings would take over. The end credits of the movie, with their foretellings of the later lives of its characters, have a terrific impact. "Only the memories and the wisps of exuberant melody are frozen in time," a critic wrote at the time. "The lives went variously on. The nostalgia may have been real enough, but it has been stripped of any easy sentimentality and it is placed in the whole setting of those lives and the country's life." The film captures a particular time and place, but it carries resonances of other towns and other summer nights.

The rightness of Lucas's casting choices has been confirmed by the later careers of his performers. For Ford, the film led to the *Star Wars* and Indiana Jones trilogies and other important starring roles. Ron Howard made the transition to further mature roles and to a major career as a director. Dreyfuss was at the beginning of his impressive career. Cindy Williams has gone on to a conspicuous career in television, and indeed, all the principal players have continued to be seen and heard.

American Graffiti confirmed the reputation of George Lucas as a first-rank American director, although it gave no hint at all of what would come next.

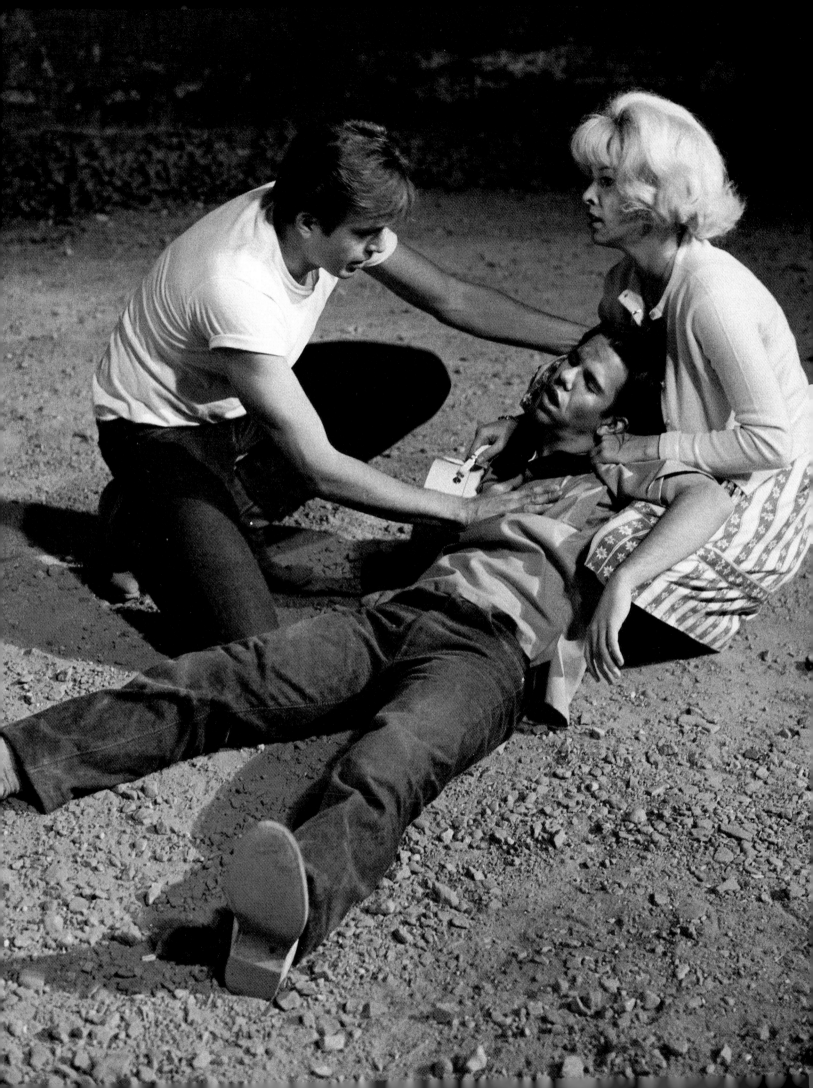

STAR WARS (1977)

Unlike many of his filmmaking contemporaries, George Lucas was not obsessively interested in the movies when he was growing up. Although he went to Saturday matinees like the other kids, his early fantasies were of being a race-car driver or a book and magazine illustrator.

But in the period following his near-fatal car crash, he started reading avidly: philosophy, history, and sociology. He discovered, significantly, the writings of Joseph Campbell about myths and their persistence through all time and all cultures.

From early folklore writings from many different cultures, Lucas devoured the great themes: epic struggles between good and evil, heroes and villains, magical princes and ogres, heroines and evil princesses, the transmission from fathers to sons of the powers of both good and evil. What the myths revealed to Lucas, among many other things, was the capacity of the human imagination to conceive alternate realities to cope with reality: figures and places and events that were before now or beyond now but were rich with meaning to our present.

The movies, with their high adventures, cliff-hanging serials, their westerns, and their swashbucklers, could be seen—in their simple and unambiguous distinctions between good and evil, heroes and villains—to be actings-out of the themes of early mythology and folklore.

Lucas's *THX 1138* had been a dark metaphor of a man inadvertently given free will, struggling to overcome the influence of an evil and oppressive state that denied self-expression. It was set in a nonspecific future and, being neither now nor then, had both a timelessness and an immediate relevance. It was saying, Lucas remarked later, that "If we're not careful about the way we conduct our lives, we're going to live in a society devoid of pain and risk, but insulated, emotionless, and much more unpleasant."

Even as he was finishing that film, Lucas told Lalo Schifrin about his ideas for his next movies. He described the project that became *American Graffiti*. "After that," Lucas said, "I want to do Flash Gordon." That was his high-concept shorthand for the undertaking that would eventually be the *Star Wars* trilogy and that would bring together his love of illustration and of the great adventure movies of his youth, and his thoughtful admiration of mythology and folklore.

The $25,000 Lucas had received for making *American Graffiti* was eaten up in the two years between the writing of the film and its reluctant release by Universal, and he was once again virtually

STAR WARS

Lucas and Mark Hamill, chatting in the setting of Luke Skywalker's home planet of Tatooine (top), both showed the strain of an exhausting production schedule.

Heading for trouble, Chewbacca, Luke Skywalker, Alec Guinness as Obi-Wan Kenobi, and Harrison Ford as Han Solo peered anxiously into the darkness.

The Millennium Falcon, Han Solo's travel-worn spaceship, whips through deep space, courtesy of the wizards of Industrial Light and Magic (opposite).

broke. Universal had first refusal on his next project but turned down his *Star Wars* idea, as did United Artists. But Alan Ladd, Jr., then a development executive at Twentieth Century-Fox, had seen a screening of *Graffiti* and was convinced it would be a huge hit. He gave Lucas $15,000 to develop a *Star Wars* script. "That was a big deal for me then," Lucas says, "because it meant I could pay off my debts and survive for the rest of the year."

"George had many permutations on the picture," Ladd said not long ago. "He once thought of it with an all-Japanese cast. He described the *kind* of picture he wanted it to be, like *Captain Blood* and so on. But it was always clear to me what he was going to do, and I never doubted that he would do it."

Lucas had written the first draft of *American Graffiti* in three weeks. The first draft of *Star Wars* took nine months, partly because he was distracted by the phenomenal success of *Graffiti* and the Academy Award nominations it received. There had been rounds of interviews and personal-appearance tours at home and abroad.

But the writing was further complicated because Lucas at first tried to cram into one script the events that eventually became the whole *Star Wars* trilogy. Having decided at last to make the first movie out of what had been the script's first act, he wrote for another six months. He did not turn in the script until the fall of 1974, a year and a half after he'd started work. Preproduction on *Star Wars* began in the spring of 1975.

The consolation prize for the long stretch of writing was that Lucas had detailed story lines for not one but three films and more general outlines for not one but three trilogies. *Star Wars, The Empire Strikes Back,* and *Return of the Jedi* are the middle trilogy, with another trilogy covering events previous to *Star Wars* and a final trilogy that would be a sequel to the three existing films. *Star Wars* is, in fact, identified in the opening credits as "Episode Four," a little-observed curiosity that could have been taken as a form of homage to the cliff-hanging Saturday serials but was, in fact, a manifestation of the grand design Lucas had conceived for his space epic.

It was Francis Coppola, during their days together on *Finian's Rainbow,* who had insisted that Lucas write his own scripts. "If you're going to be a director, you've got to be a writer, for your own protection," Lucas says Coppola told him.

As he was writing *Star Wars,* Lucas began to react to an unusual response from *Graffiti.* "I was getting hundreds and hundreds of letters, from kids especially, that were very positive, telling me how dramatically the film had changed their lives." He

had been disappointed that *THX 1138* had been coolly received. Now the mail reconvinced him that movies could make a difference.

With the new film, Lucas says, he wanted to do a kind of fairy tale. "There was no modern mythology to give kids a sense of values, to give them a strong mythological fantasy life. Westerns were the last of that genre for Americans. Nothing was being done for young people that had real psychological underpinnings and was aimed at intelligent beings." Although Coppola was urging him to drop the project for a more serious film, like *Apocalypse Now,* Lucas elected to follow his own stars. "I decided I'd go for the less chic route." Coppola went off to do *Apocalypse* himself.

Amazingly, the original budget for *Star Wars* was only $3.5 million, although inflation had doubled it to $7 million even before production began. It was then $9.5 million and the film went $3 million over budget because of the high cost of creating a nonexistent world. (Lucas recalled years later that a million dollars had been spent for special effects, but to that point not a frame had been shot.) The eventual cost of the effects was $2.5 million, still extremely modest by the standards of that day and this.

Lucas recruited a remarkable creative team, most of whom were to work with him often thereafter. John Barry was the production designer, Ralph McQuarrie the illustrator, Norman Reynolds and Leslie Dilley the art directors, Stuart Freeborn in charge of makeup. John Dykstra supervised the photographic effects, John Stears the production and mechanical effects.

Lucas's line producer, Gary Kurtz, hired as production supervisor Robert Watts, who had had the same function on Stanley Kubrick's *2001: A Space Odyssey.* Watts had begun his career as a gofer and rose through the ranks as second and then first assistant director. He was to work with Lucas for fourteen years, ultimately as supervisor of European production for Lucasfilm.

"We were in a stop-and-go situation," Watts remembers. "We were supposed to start shooting in March 1976, but we didn't get the final go-ahead until New Year's Day. It's amazing that we got it together. We had a thirteen-week shooting schedule and we went three weeks over — *only* three weeks.

"The pressures on George were enormous. He'd only done small pictures before, all on location. Here we were using every stage at one studio, Elstree, and a large stage at another studio, Shepperton. We kept waiting for matte plates from Los Angeles, but they never showed up. It turned out to be a lucky thing in the end; we never tried it again." Hired for the one film, Watts worked on all six of the *Star Wars* and Indiana Jones films.

The **Sand People** (left), also known as the **Tusken Raiders**, were nomadic and villainous creatures on Tatooine, a desert planet, filmed in Tunisia.

Captured by the Jawas, another set of villains, **R2-D2** and **C-3PO** are stuck amid the innards of the **Sand Crawler**, one of those settings where the imaginations of Lucas and his team could run amok.

Two indelible Lucas creations, C-3PO (Anthony Daniels)
and R2-D2 (Kenny Baker), wait out a tense moment in a
passageway on Princess Leia's ship, Tantive IV.

"I suppose it's space fantasy," Lucas said at the time. "But we don't explain anything. We take all the hardware for granted. The story really is an action adventure, a fantasy hero's journey. It's aimed primarily at teenagers, the same audience as *American Graffiti*."

On the film's production notes, Lucas quoted from the preface Sir Arthur Conan Doyle wrote for his non-Holmes novel, *The Lost World*:

> I have wrought my simple plan
> If I give one hour of joy
> To the boy who's half a man
> Or the man who's half a boy.

The outreach of *Star Wars* has obviously gone far beyond teenagers, or men and boys. It has proved to be an all-ages adventure, with distinctive characteristics that were different from anything that had been attempted before.

There was, most especially, Lucas's emphasis on the idea of a *used* future, a future that was meant to be experienced as reality rather than fantasy. The *Star Wars* future was not showroom shiny but dented and rusty, as if it had had hard use on the back roads of innumerable galaxies. Lucas told an interviewer during production in England that the Apollo capsules may have looked brand-new when they soared away, but it was clear when they returned that the interior was littered with candy wrappers, empty Tang cans, and other trash, just like the family station wagon.

Ben Burtt was a teaching assistant in the sound department of the cinema school at USC when he was recruited to join Lucas on *Star Wars*. At their first conference, Burtt says, Lucas told him he wanted everything to sound *real:* "the motors to sound real, to sound squeaky and rusty, to use acoustic sounds—that is, to go off in the world and gather sounds. By using them, as we discovered, everything begins to take on a sense of reality. The spaceships sound like they really have motors in them."

Burtt spent a whole year collecting sounds the way other men collect butterflies or matchbooks. "I'd call up somebody and say, 'I hear you have a trained bear that makes a funny sound.' I'd watch the Army blow up planes with missiles, go out on an aircraft carrier with my tape recorder." He built a library of thousands of cross-indexed sounds that he could then mix or process to give Lucas whatever he needed, from the whack of a punch in the face to the grinding of a rusty motor or an airplane exploding.

Harrison Ford, back to carpentry after *American Graffiti*, first

STAR WARS

The horned Bantha, a creature used as a pack animal by the Tusken Raiders, was in truth an elephant in disguise.

(overleaf) In a cavernous hangar, one of the extra-ordinary sets created for *Star Wars*, the rebel pilots (the good guys) prepare their fighter craft for battle with the Empire.

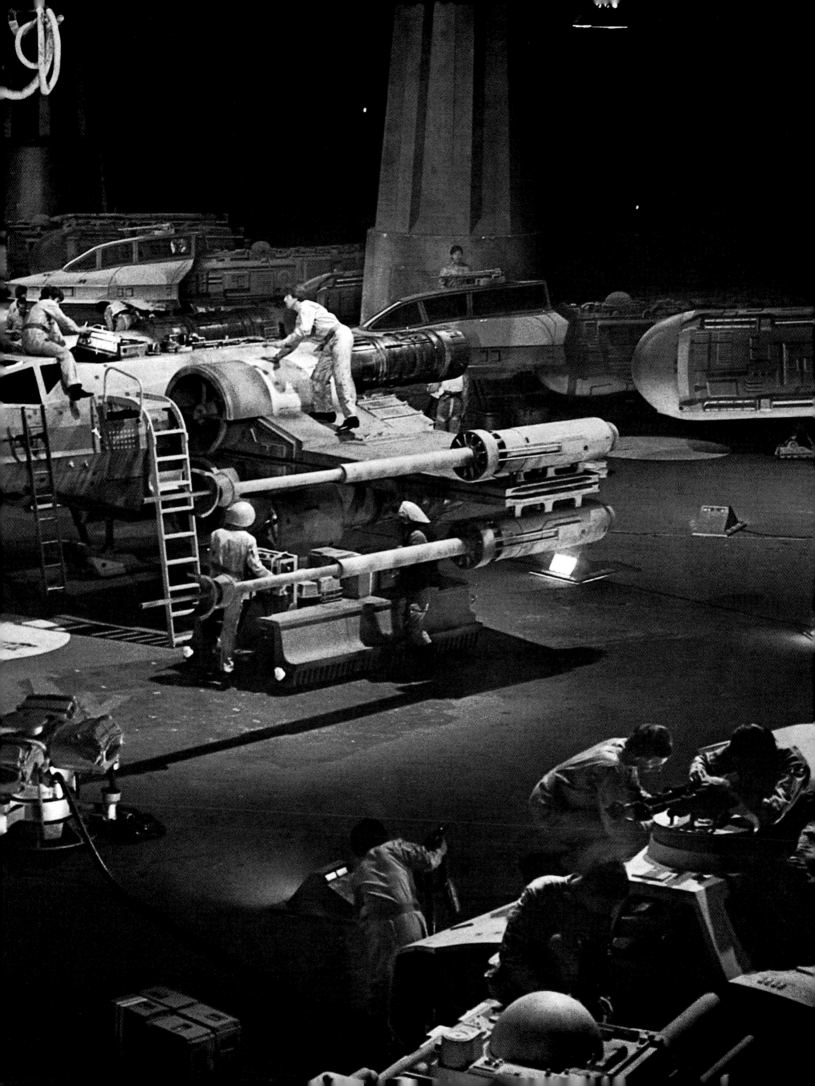

heard that none of the members of that cast were going to be considered for *Star Wars*. Fred Roos, consulting on casting as he had on *Graffiti*, says, "I urged Harrison as Han Solo from the first git-go, but even though he'd worked with him, George didn't know him very well." Ford was asked to read with other actors.

"Finally, they made me an offer," Ford says, "and this was promoted as a low-budget movie. It certainly was for actors; I can attest to that," he adds with a sly grin. Lucas later assigned percentages of the film's profits to his principal actors. "We ended up earning what we were worth," says Ford.

Carrie Fisher was nineteen when she was cast as Princess Leia, and it took her a while to be sure Lucas wouldn't change his mind. "I always felt I had the most *arch* dialogue to say. In my first scene I had to say to Peter Cushing, 'Oh, Governor Tarkin, I thought I recognized your foul stench when I came aboard.' What I really wanted to say, in effect, was 'OmiGod I came on board and there was this smell, and of course it turns out to be you.' That would've been closer to my personality. But George took me aside and said, 'This is all very real and very serious.' *Right.* I'd have done anything I was told because I thought they'd figure out soon enough that they hadn't hired someone attractive enough, and they'd fire me. When they hired me, they told me to lose ten pounds. At my height that's like asking me to lose a leg. So I kept thinking I'd show up on the stage and they'd say, 'Okay, tubby, we're going to go with a thinner person who's, you know, more *sparkly* than you.'

"But George wanted and hired strong personalities. He said that was his way to go. Between the three of us that was a lot of personality in one spaceship, in one galaxy. Harrison used to say, 'You can type this stuff but you can't say it.' All the navigational stuff. I'd have to say, 'I have placed information vital to the survival of the rebellion in the memory system of this R2-D2 so my father will know how to retrieve it.' I mean, c'mon. But I have an abruptness in my demeanor, and I suppose it fit. I always feel that George put me on whatever map I'm located on, so he can ask me to do pretty much what he wants, but don't tell him that."

Mark Hamill, who was to become Luke Skywalker and the third of the *Star Wars* triumvirate, went to a dual audition. "Brian De Palma was casting for *Carrie*. I assumed that the quiet chap sitting beside him was his assistant." It was, of course, Lucas, and after the audition Lucas sent him some pages of the script and had him back for a videotaped audition. "That was the first time I met Harrison. I remember thinking that he must be the Flash Gordon character and I must be one of the sidekicks."

The title of the full script, as Hamill recalls, was *The Adventures of Luke Skywalker as Taken from the Journal of the Whills: Saga One: The Star Wars*. "I remember George saying, 'This is the most expensive low-budget film ever made.' That was the spirit, and something I'll never forget. Everything on the first one had a breeziness and a freedom that we never had again. Sometimes a director's first films are the most exciting in their lives because after that the pressures increase exponentially. George looked harried. He was already under great pressure."

Hamill was twenty-four when shooting on *Star Wars* began in 1975, thirty-two when *Return of the Jedi* was released in 1983. "I played the same character all the time, but it was at different stages in his life, and in mine." Hamill has continued to be successful in films and television, but his greatest pleasures have come on the Broadway stage, where he starred in *Amadeus* and other plays.

The stirring *Star Wars* theme, reverberating through all three films, has become one of the most widely identifiable pieces of film music since the *Gone with the Wind* theme. The composer John Williams remembers that Steven Spielberg, for whom he had done *Jaws*, recommended him to Lucas. They met in Lucas's small office at Universal before shooting began. Lucas wasted no words. "It's kind of a space-y film," Lucas said. "Would you like to do the music?" Williams said, "I'd love to," and so began their association.

The two men later spent three days at Lucas's home in San Anselmo, viewing the picture on a Moviola and deciding where music should go. Lucas had put some Dvořák and Wagner on a temporary music track; and it was clear that he wanted a nineteenth-century classical sound. Lucas's reasoning, Williams says, "was that we were going to see planets unseen, creatures we hadn't met before. Everything visual was going to be unfamiliar, and that, therefore, what should be familiar was the emotional connection that the film has through the ear to the viscera. This I have to credit George with, the idea of making the music, as the composer would say, solidly tonal and clearly melodic, acoustic rather than electronic."

STAR WARS

In a now-legendary visual sequence (opposite top), Darth Vader in his Tie fighter streaks down the narrow Death Star trench in pursuit of Luke Skywalker's X-wing.

Lending his imposing dignity to the story and the film, Alec Guinness as Obi-Wan Kenobi is the wise and weary counselor to the tousled Luke Skywalker.

Williams told him, "Why don't you let me write our own classic music, and develop themes of our own so we won't be violating great works of art from the past. I can take my theme and do it slowly, quickly, up a third, down a fourth, bend it around, attenuate it, and so forth." Williams laughs and says, "It's very challenging when someone says to a composer, 'do a score like Wagner.'"

Williams also proposed to Lucas what he calls the "leitmotif" approach—distinctive themes for the Princess, Luke, Han, Darth Vader, and the robots. Lucas agreed. Williams went off to compose, and they next met on the scoring stage at Denham Studios in England, with the London Symphony ready to go.

From the recording stage, Lucas phoned Spielberg in Los Angeles and let him hear a half-hour of the score. Spielberg now remembers telling Lucas that it depressed him terribly. "George said, 'Why?' I said, 'Because John's supposed to do *Close Encounters* for me and he's just spent his last dollar for you.' But the truth was John had a lot of dollars left for me." The score for *Star Wars* won an Oscar.

Lucas has been quoted as saying, "Technology won't save us," which is a statement about the world but no less a statement about movies. If a movie is not driven by its basic story and the characters who populate it, all the special effects you can dream up won't save it, as several science-fiction films have proved in the years since *Star Wars*. Lucas's story was surefire.

As critics noted, the movie had elements of the western and the swashbuckler as well as Flash Gordon. "The sidekicks," I wrote at the time, "are salty squatty robots instead of leathery old cowpokes who scratch their whiskers and say 'Aw shucks' a lot, and the gunfighters square off with laser swords instead of Colt revolvers. But it is all and gloriously one, the mythic and simple world of the good guys vs. the bad guys, the rustlers and the land grabbers, the old generation saving the young with a last heroic gesture, which drives home the message of courage and conviction. There are inspirations from other movie forms, including the swashbuckler with its captive and endangered princess, the monster film with its creatures both good and evil, and almost any form with its second male lead wavering between cynicism and idealism but making the right choice in the very nick of time."

Still, it was the extraordinary abundance of visual and aural

STAR WARS

Kidnapped by the Jawas, R2-D2 and C-3PO are marched aboard the Sand Crawler in one of the film's serial-like successions of cliff-hangers.

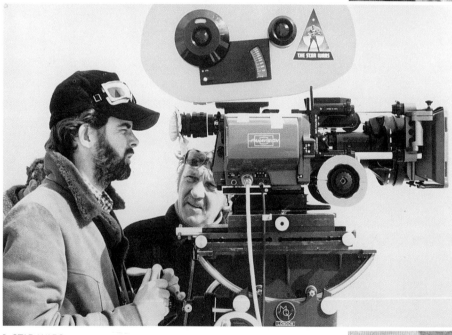

STAR WARS

One of Darth Vader's spear-carrying storm troopers (top) rides a prehistoric beast called a Dewback to confront our heroes.

Consulting with camera operator Ronnie Taylor, Lucas checks the composition of a shot (above). *Star Wars* was to be the last film Lucas would direct personally, preferring thereafter to create stories and serve as executive producer.

Riding the camera dolly (opposite), Lucas follows the action as Han Solo, Luke Skywalker, and Chewbacca head toward the grand award ceremony at the end of *Star Wars.*

special effects that lifted the film past anything that had been done before. There were seventy individuals and five firms listed in the end credits for miniature- and optical-effects work alone, in addition to the four dozen creators cited elsewhere in the credits. (The cast list was a mere two dozen names long.) John Dykstra had recruited a team that included a dozen model makers alone, men like Steven Gawley and Lorne Peterson who, nearly twenty years later, are still making models at ILM.

The computer, and specifically the computer-driven camera, which could repeat its movements exactly and endlessly, were central to the revolution in special effects that *Star Wars* represented. Pieces of film could be run through the camera several times, adding an additional image with each passage and making possible those amazing starship dogfights, in which everything in the scene is moving at once. It was a far cry from the single giant ship moving majestically through silent and motionless space. It was the year's most razzle-dazzling family movie.

It was indeed a phenomenon, one of that handful of movies, historically speaking, that transcend the business to become a news event and a sociological phenomenon. *Star Wars* lured everyone—teenager or not, regular filmgoer or not—and the faithful went to see it again and again.

There had been relatively little prepublicity about *Star Wars,* partly because the studio itself had only the vaguest clues as to what the finished movie would look like. But the word had got out to the science-fiction and fantasy enthusiasts. On the Wednesday in May 1977 when *Star Wars* opened, there were lines around the block. Lucas himself was in Los Angeles, overseeing the sound mix on one of the foreign versions of the film. He and his wife went to a restaurant across Hollywood Boulevard from Grauman's Chinese Theater. "It was like a mob scene. One lane of traffic was blocked off. There were police there. There were limousines in front of the theater. There were lines, eight or nine people *wide,* going both ways and around the block. I said, 'My God, what's going on here? It must be a premiere or something.' I looked at the marquee, and it was *Star Wars.*" It became the box-office hit of the year and remains the second-biggest hit of all time.

Lucas had shrewdly retained the sequel rights to the story and the characters, and he had negotiated away from Fox most of the merchandising rights. The novelization of the script alone sold more than three million copies. He was unlikely ever to be broke again. But the making of the film had also brought home some momentous lessons to him. Carrie Fisher remembers an evening on the mixing stage during postproduction. "George was lying on

the couch, and he'd been up for something like thirty-six hours. They were threatening to take the film out of his hands, cut the negative, and go right to the theaters. And he looked up at me and said, 'I don't ever want to do this again.'"

Even during the shooting in England, Lucas told a visitor, "I know I'm much more a filmmaker than a movie director. My personal attitudes are just not prone to this kind of gigantic enterprise. I like being a captain in the trenches rather than a general in headquarters. When the budget goes beyond $2 or $3 million [this was 1976] another law takes over. You lose the personal touch, the personal contact with every aspect of the movie—unless you're a Kubrick, who can take all the time that's required to oversee all the details yourself. You become more remote than I like to be."

Just from his earnings from *American Graffiti,* Lucas said, he could, by living modestly, never have to earn another dime as long as he lived. (Coppola was given 10 percent of the film's profits for his participation. His biographer, Peter Cowie, says Coppola earned $3 million. Lucas, as became his custom, assigned a considerable percentage of his participation to key associates in the cast and on the crew. He has very likely created at least a dozen millionaires.) The sudden wealth meant that he could, if he wished, retreat to private life in northern California and make the kind of special experimental and cinema-verité films he had started to do at USC.

But life refused to be that simple. For one thing, Lucas was worried that the great technicians of special effects—like the matte artists Peter Ellenshaw of Disney and Al Whitlock of Universal whom he had recruited to work on *Star Wars*—were a vanishing breed. The big pictures themselves might be impossible to do in another twenty years, for want of the skilled artists who made the magic. Encouraging those artists and helping to inspire and sustain a new generation of wizards was part of the vision he and Coppola had had almost a decade earlier: the dream of a preproduction and postproduction facility where the filmmakers, in every sense, called the shots. For the moment, Lucas was not simply a success, he was a phenomenon. What was certain was that he could do almost anything he wanted to do—except retreat to a quiet, private world of experimental film.

STAR WARS

Making film history, Lucas guides the making of *Star Wars* in London in 1976 as Chewbacca (actor Peter Mayhew in a furry suit) towers over him.

MORE AMERICAN GRAFFITI (1979)

"The focus of my life, the thing I care about, was and is making movies: writing and shooting and editing films," Lucas has said. "And what sustains you through a time of poverty, which was the first ten years, also sustains you in a time of wealth. You're so busy being creative that you don't have time to do a lot of stupid things. There's never been a period when money was a major focus for me."

Even so, the financial success of *American Graffiti* followed by the even greater financial success of *Star Wars* imposed changes on Lucas's life. The dream of a self-contained filmmaking enterprise, separated geographically and philosophically from Hollywood, was suddenly nearer to hand. Achieving it meant, however, that Lucas would have to give up some of the hands-on writing, producing, and directing and become a special kind of creative mogul.

In fact, Lucas had no choice but to turn over some of his creative responsibilities. As a consequence of his success, he was involved with two sequels simultaneously. One of them was the second *Star Wars* film, *The Empire Strikes Back,* the other a sequel to *American Graffiti.* Lucas had agreed to a three-picture deal with Universal when he signed to do the original, and now the studio, not unnaturally, wanted a sequel. (The third project was an original called "Radioland Murders," a script Lucas had been tinkering with for years and that was finally produced in 1994.)

For *More American Graffiti,* Lucas turned to a young writer-director named B. W. L. (Bill) Norton, who had made his reputation with a film called *Cisco Pike,* a 1971 drug-culture story starring Gene Hackman and Kris Kristofferson.

"George had seen *Cisco Pike* and liked it," Norton says. "He'd also read some of my other scripts. *Cisco* has developed a cult following, but at the time it put me out of directing for eight years, and so I wrote.

"When he started work on *More American Graffiti,* George wanted someone about his own age—I'm just a year older than he is—and somebody with a California background to write the

MORE AMERICAN GRAFFITI

In 1964, the *Graffiti* gang meet again, with Charles Martin Smith as Terry the Toad, due to ship out for Vietnam the next day, and Cindy Williams and Ron Howard expecting their first child.

script, and I'm a Californian." Norton had been in film school at UCLA when Lucas was at USC.

"We talked, and I asked him what the chances were of my directing. He said that, if he liked the script, I could direct it."

As was to become his custom, Lucas would be the executive producer on the film, with his USC classmate Howard Kazanjian as line producer. Lucas, Kazanjian, and Norton met in San Anselmo to thrash out major lines of the script.

"Some of the stories George had already worked out in detail, others needed fixing," Norton says. "But he knew that Ron Howard and Cindy Williams were going to be caught up in campus demonstrations and so on. I was impressed by the insights he had to the characters, and the back stories he could give the actors about the characters."

Although it was to be, by definition, a mainstream, major-studio picture, Lucas thought that *More American Graffiti* could be experimental in its own way, pushing still further the idea of having several fragmented story lines, the technique he had used in the original film.

"I thought the fragmented technique would be a good way to tell a story about the 60s," Lucas says. It was a film about the Vietnam War, and Lucas wanted to make it a documentary-style satire on the war—a *Dr. Strangelove* technique he had once envisioned for *Apocalypse Now* before Coppola took it in quite a different direction. Lucas used the approach in *More American Graffiti,* personally photographing and editing some of the battle scenes (shot in Stockton, California).

In lieu of a summer's night, *More American Graffiti* centers on a succession of New Year's Eves, starting in 1964, two years after the gang finished high school. (The narrative cuts back and forth among the New Year's Eves.) When first seen, Ron Howard and Cindy Williams are expecting their first child. Paul Le Mat is still racing cars. Charlie Martin Smith as Toad is in uniform, shipping out the next day for Vietnam. Candy Clark is living with a self-centered and spaced-out guitar player. The voice of the unseen Wolfman Jack remains a kind of Greek chorus on the events, and as before, there is a wall-to-wall collage of period songs from Simon and Garfunkel, Bob Dylan, and many groups.

The visual style is highly innovative, with the screen occasionally dividing into two, three, six, or more windows, presenting fragments of several stories simultaneously, or different angles on the same event or, Andy Warhol-like, a dozen identical images.

Propelling the action are four major story strands. One is a peace demonstration in which Williams and Howard (their marriage

MORE AMERICAN GRAFFITI

Paul Le Mat (opposite) has advanced from his souped-up roadster to the costly and dangerous hot-rod crazy cars in the dark, sobering sequel to *American Graffiti*.

In *More American Graffiti*, the Vietnam War and campus riots, vividly recreated in the film (top), have replaced the innocence of high school days. Here, Terry escapes from a helicopter crash in the Vietnam jungle.

Briefly photographing again, Lucas personally watches over the Vietnam sequences (shot near Stockton, California) and rides along on a helicopter shot.

now fraying under the stresses of three young children) are inadvertently trapped. Their love is rekindled, and they are, the viewer guesses, radicalized by the experience. Toad, surviving some horrendous battle experiences in 'Nam but still harassed by a drunken officer, is at last preparing to go AWOL by walking away from the war. The battle sequences, including a down-and-dirty football game played in the mud, come as close to reflecting the GI's actual existence in Vietnam as any film has.

Candy Clark, her faithless guitarist no longer in her life, falls in with a rock group (and helps precipitate a colossal brawl in the great western tradition). Le Mat is doing ever better at the track and has a charming encounter with a beautiful Icelandic visitor who has not a word of English. But there are tip-offs that neither he nor Toad will survive the last New Year's Eve in 1967. The world has grown significantly darker.

"My whole idea of a style for *More American Graffiti* was ultimately unsuccessful, I guess," Lucas said later. "Bill's a more conservative kind of storyteller, and I think I forced him to do things that in his heart he wasn't comfortable with."

But as Norton himself sees it, looking back, "Multiple stories are very risky. They worked well in *American Graffiti* because there was unity of time and place. But in *More American Graffiti* we were asking a lot of the audience because things were happening at different times, as well as in different places. But there are still scenes I'm very proud of and stylistic things I like a lot. And George was very generous and courteous. He came and watched, but he let me direct."

Despite its often raucous comedy and some affectingly romantic moments, *More American Graffiti* was not a big success. Its embracing vision was not so comfortably nostalgic as in the original film. Yet the sequel, seen a dozen years later, is an engrossing record of a turbulent decade, with its cacophonous mixture of flower power, new music, social protest, and the horrors of war.

MORE AMERICAN GRAFFITI

The antiwar riots (opposite) that erupted in the 60s embroiled the Ron Howard and Cindy Williams characters and, radicalizing them, shored up a shaky marriage.

Reflecting still other elements of the flower-powered 60s Candy Clark (top) has been fleeing a rough relationship with a guitarist when she runs into a rock group in a wrecked van.

One of the band members urges her to try out as a singer with the group. Like others, but not all of the high school gang, she manages a happy ending in difficult times.

THE EMPIRE STRIKES BACK (1980)

The almost impossible challenge of *The Empire Strikes Back* was to out-spectacle *Star Wars*. Steven Gawley, who joined Lucasfilm to work as a model maker on *Star Wars* just as he left Cal State Long Beach, said not long ago, "Each time you have a project and the audience sees it and believes it, you're preparing them to expect even more. So the next time out they're more sophisticated, and you've got to be more sophisticated in what you do. They'll spot bad stuff, old-fashioned process shots and rear projection, in a minute."

The Empire Strikes Back had something like twice as many special-effects shots as *Star Wars.* One sequence — in which Harrison Ford's "Millennium Falcon" starship flies into a meteorite field to elude the pursuing rebel ships — required no fewer than two hundred pieces of film and a week just to run and rerun the various pieces of film into one.

Warren Franklin began as an assistant in the optical department when Industrial Light and Magic moved from Van Nuys to San Rafael, California, in 1979, just as work on *The Empire Strikes Back* began. He remembers that "the biggest challenge we faced were the snow scenes on the ice planet Hoth. The traditional blue-screen techniques and the new ones we developed for *Star Wars* were all done against black space, which was very forgiving in terms of matte lines around the spaceships and generally making things look real. It was as if George had come up with the most difficult thing to do — absolutely — outside of water, which he always avoided, thankfully."

As production began, ILM was still completing the move north. "I remember sitting in the optical department, as boxes and boxes of film piled up, and not having any way to put it together because we were still waiting to complete the optical printer. I don't think we ever quite knew if we were going to make it or not," says Franklin, who is now a consultant to Lucasfilm, having risen to head ILM and the other support divisions.

Ted Moehnke, who first worked for Lucas as a prop man on *THX 1138,* recalls that a swamp scene in *Empire,* in which a monster shoots out of the swamp hoping to grab R2-D2, was actually shot in Lucas's unfinished swimming pool in San Rafael. "We piled the whole crew in the pool, which was filled with muddy water, and George shot the footage himself. Lot of fun!"

Audiences were awed by (but expected nothing less from) such gee-whiz sequences as the gallumphing approach across the snow of mastodon-like robots. They were actually models a few feet

THE EMPIRE STRIKES BACK

The wise and sad-eyed Yoda (opposite), one of the most endearing of the Lucas creations, was brought to life by Frank Oz, who did the same for Miss Piggy.

Lando Calrissian (Billy Dee Williams) and Princess Leia (Carrie Fisher) commiserate with Han Solo (above) just before he's dumped into the Carbon-Freezing Chamber.

high, photographed in laborious stop-motion, the footage then printed with film of actual actors charging through real snow.

Lucas had reassembled many from the *Star Wars* team, including Norman Reynolds as the production designer and Ralph McQuarrie as the illustrator. To direct the film's ever more complex mixture of live action and effects, Lucas recruited Irvin Kershner, who had directed an earlier sequel, *The Return of a Man Called Horse*, which Lucas thought was even better than the original. Lucas was again executive producer, with his USC schoolmate and longtime friend and associate Gary Kurtz as line producer. The production supervisor again, as he had been on *Star Wars*, was Robert Watts, who held the title of associate producer.

Kershner remembers a first discussion about the project in

Lucas's house in San Anselmo. "He took me into a workroom, and on the walls were the plans for Skywalker Ranch. He said, 'This is why we're making the second one. If it works, I'll build this. If it works, we'll not only build it, we'll make more *Star Wars*! If it doesn't work, it's over!'" Lucas added that he was financing the film himself, which Kershner felt put even more responsibility on his shoulders as director.

The veteran Leigh Brackett had done a first draft of *Empire*, based on Lucas's story, and then she died of cancer. Lucas and Spielberg had already hired a young writer named Lawrence Kasdan to write the script for *Raiders of the Lost Ark*. Now Lucas asked Kasdan to take over the revisions of *The Empire Strikes Back*.

With the Empire's forces approaching, the rebel fighters rush through the Transport Bay to begin the evacuation of the ice planet Hoth, where the Skywalker team has been regrouping (opposite).

The director as conductor, Irvin Kershner in a silhouette gestures a suggestion to Peter Mayhew as Chewbacca.

"I'd taken the *Raiders* script up to him in Marin," Kasdan remembered later, "and I said, 'Don't you want to read this first?' George said, 'Well, if I hate it tonight, I'll call you up and take back this offer. But I just get a feeling about people.' And it's true, he does. In a lot of ways, George has been an important mentor to me. His ideas have been important to me, and I'm still trying to operate on those principles." One of the principles is giving key participants in a film a share of the profits. Kasdan was paid relatively little for the script, but his share of the profits has amounted to a lot of money.

Kershner took part in long story conferences with Lucas and Kasdan in San Anselmo. When the script was finished, Kershner created a series of shot-by-shot sketches for the film that finally amounted to a book nine inches thick. There were sixty-four different sets, plus location shooting in Norway, which doubled for the ice planet Hoth, where the rebels, including Princess Leia and her pals, were hiding from the evil Empire.

Kershner left a duplicate copy of the book of sketches with Lucas. "I could call him in California and say, 'George, Number 2FBL, I'm going to make it more foreground.' Or whatever." In lieu of daily rushes, Lucas received a black-and-white videocassette of the footage, made as it ran through an editing machine.

"Talk about confidence!" Kershner said recently.

The value of the dollar fell sharply against the pound, and Kershner warned Lucas that they were going over budget, since it now took more dollars to pay the English salaries and services. "George said, 'Keep right on going the way you're going,'" Kershner says. "George showed some early scenes to a banker in Boston and borrowed enough more money to finish the film.

"People think that because it was a sequel and we had the same major cast, I had no freedom. I had tremendous freedom, and it's to George's credit."

The Empire Strikes Back was another huge success at the box office—and with critics, who are accustomed to thinking that no sequel can be as good as the original. The effects were brilliant. Even the laser-sword play was achieved in a new and subtly more realistic way. Yet, as before, all the incandescent effects were, as Lucas likes to say, story driven and not ends in themselves. However splendid they were to watch, they were advancing a suspenseful story.

The characters, cynical Han Solo, idealistic Luke Skywalker, feisty Princess Leia, were more interesting psychologically than before, inspired in their triangular bantering (it may be) by such classic threesomes as Clark Gable, Spencer Tracy, and Myrna Loy in *Test Pilot*.

"This was the least resolved of the three," Robert Watts says. "You knew there had to be another act. It was also the darkest of the three. There was a chance to give depth to the characters."

Indeed the new film felt, even more than the first, like part of a much larger tapestry. It was identified in the opening titles as "Episode Five," and its ending, ingeniously, was both a satisfying conclusion and a cliff-hanger that left one of the trio in calamitous trouble. That structure, and the debut of Yoda, the wise and sad-eyed old party counseling Luke Skywalker, confirmed the richness of Lucas's imagination. Yoda, whom one critic characterized as a light-year leprechaun, was operated by the same Frank Oz who was the voice and maneuverer of Miss Piggy.

Like all fine fantasies, *The Empire Strikes Back* has the quality of a parable on good and evil and the moral imperatives of hard work, determination, and idealism. And it seemed clear then, as it does now, that its positive and uplifting tone had a lot to do, possibly in a subliminal way, with the popularity of the film. For all the special effects, the story, at heart, was man against man, or man against beast. The human element was, as in all times, what finally counted.

THE EMPIRE STRIKES BACK

In a spectacular action sequence, the Empire warriors storm the rebels' command center, but the rebels have escaped (opposite). Director Irvin Kershner (above) was snow-coated in Norway's freezing weather.

THE EMPIRE STRIKES BACK

The masked and deep-voiced Darth Vader (top) is a fearsome figure in his cape—a once and future black knight out of Lucas's myth-inspired imagination.

A futuristic sword fight with lightsabers (the light added in postproduction with some special-effects magic) pitted Luke against the dreaded Darth Vader (above).

In yet another mind-boggling set, this one at the heart of Cloud City, Darth Vader beckons to Luke, who could certainly use a helping hand, though preferably not that one.

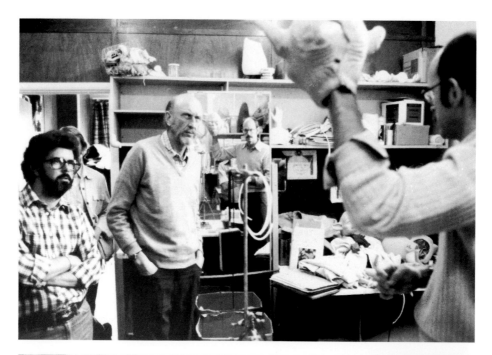

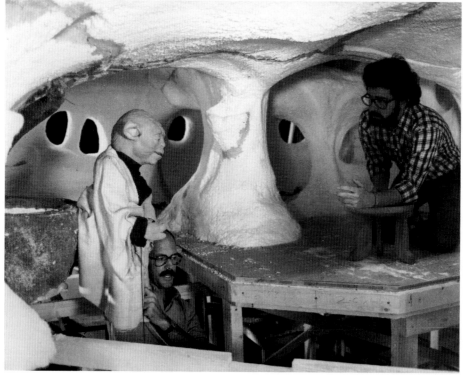

THE EMPIRE STRIKES BACK

Bringing Yoda alive, puppeteer/Muppeteer Frank Oz (top) shows director Irvin Kershner and Lucas how Yoda will look in action. Within the set of Yoda's house (above), Oz pokes head and arm through a false floor and rehearses the scene while Lucas checks the camera angle.

THE EMPIRE STRIKES BACK

Meeting Yoda, Hamill as Luke Skywalker, damp from a plunge in the swamp, gets some wise and kindly advice from the timeless creature.

THE EMPIRE STRIKES BACK

The giant Walkers (opposite), resembling mechanized mastodons, lead the Empire's advance across blizzardy fields of the ice planet Hoth toward the rebel encampment.

More wild weaponry, a ray gun created for the film is mounted on a kind of intergalactic snowmobile (top).

Designer and model maker Phil Tippett animates the Walkers for the stop-motion camera to create film that will be printed with live-action footage. The result is the composite on the facing page.

THE EMPIRE STRIKES BACK

Cast and crew work in zero-degree weather as Norway becomes the ice planet Hoth, where Luke Skywalker and his pals hide out from the revenge-seeking Empire. The giant Tauntaun at right was another of the fantastical creations for the film.

KAGEMUSHA or THE SHADOW WARRIOR (1980)

Lucas and Coppola are both great admirers of the Japanese master filmmaker Akira Kurosawa. His films include, among many others, *Rashomon, Ikiru, Seven Samurai* (which became the model for the American film *The Magnificent Seven*), *Dodes 'Ka-Den*, and *Dersu Uzala*, all shown internationally to admiring audiences.

Yet in 1980 Lucas discovered that Kurosawa was having trouble raising enough financing to shoot his present project, a Samurai film on an epic scale called *Kagemusha* or *The Shadow Warrior*. Although *Dersu Uzala* had won the Academy Award as best foreign film in 1975, Kurosawa had been unable to make a film since.

"I went to Laddie [Alan Ladd, Jr.] at Fox," Lucas says, "and, using the power I had because of the success of *Star Wars*, I got them to put up half the money for Kurosawa to finish the film. I asked Francis to join me." Lucas and Coppola were credited as executive producers on the international version of the film.

Kurosawa's battle scenes, whether of man against man or of armies against armies, are one of his trademarks, and in *Kagemusha* he outdid himself. It is the story of a foot soldier who, because of their close physical resemblance, is persuaded to impersonate a great warlord, with fateful consequences. Horsemen in brilliant costumes of the period thunder across dusty fields and even go clattering down the steps of castle battlements. The film won first prize, the Palme d'Or, at the Cannes Film Festival. Kurosawa was then seventy-one, but the film had the vigor of a young man's work. Its success enabled Kurosawa to find a French producer to finance his next film, his own interpretation of Shakespeare's *King Lear*, called *Ran*—the same basic story except that the king/warlord has sons bad and good instead of daughters bad and good.

Lucas later introduced Kurosawa to Spielberg, who helped him mount *Dreams*, an almost surrealistic dramatization of some of Kurosawa's fantasies. ILM did the special effects for the film.

"There is a whole group of us who have a strong wish to help others," Lucas says, "either young directors who haven't yet had a shot at it, or older directors who've been passed by but who still have creative ideas."

KAGEMUSHA

The striking pageantry of warfare in medieval Japan, often a feature of Akira Kurosawa's films, found vivid expression in his film about a common man who becomes the double for a warrior leader.

On location in Japan during the making of *Kagemusha* (opposite), Coppola and Lucas, executive producers of the international version of the film, met with Kurosawa and an interpreter.

RAIDERS OF THE LOST ARK (1981)

The week *Star Wars* opened, Lucas invited his friend Steven Spielberg to join him on vacation in Hawaii. "We both have a tradition that, when we have a film opening for which there are high expectations, we get out of town," Spielberg has explained.

Spielberg had first met Lucas at a student-film festival at UCLA, which Lucas won with "THX 1138:4EB." There was no time for more than a quick handshake, although Spielberg says he had no doubt that he had seen the work of a major filmmaker-to-be.

"George was this very, very young, very droll Ewok. Make that a Pre-wok," Spielberg says, laughing. "He was somewhat Yoda-like. Although Francis was the inspiration for all film students then, George came across as the young seer. He seemed to have all the wisdom, although Francis was doing all the doing." Over the next years the two men became close friends.

Before he went to Hawaii, Lucas had glimpsed the opening-night crowds for *Star Wars,* but nevertheless his expectations for the film were not high. Science-fiction or fantasy films were out of vogue, and this film's appeal, Lucas thought, was limited to the young. "He wrote a prediction on a matchbook that it would only do $16 million," Spielberg says. "I went to a highbrow screening—Fellini's *Amarcord,* I think—and when the trailer for *Star Wars* was shown, it was booed," Spielberg remembers. "You had to think, well, it'll never get *that* crowd."

But as he and Spielberg sat on the beach in Hawaii, Lucas went off to take a call from Los Angeles. The word was that the first screenings of *Star Wars* had completely sold out all over the country. "George was in a state of euphoria," Spielberg says.

Lucas asked Spielberg what he was going to do next. "I said I wanted to do a James Bond film," Spielberg says. "United Artists approached me after *Sugarland Express* and asked me to do a film for them. I said, 'sure, give me the next James Bond film.' But they said they couldn't do that. Then George said he had a film that was even better than a James Bond. It was called *Raiders of*

the *Lost Ark,* and it was about this archaeologist-adventurer who goes searching for the Ark of the Covenant. When he mentioned that it would be like the old serials and that the guy would wear a soft fedora and carry a bullwhip, I was completely hooked. George said, 'Are you interested?' and I said, 'I want to direct it,' and he said, 'It's yours.'"

Lucas had started thinking about Indiana Jones as early as 1970. "I wanted to do an adventure serials that had the same impact and pace as the old serials used to have," he says. The idea of making the central figure an archaeologist grew out of courses in anthropology Lucas took at Modesto Junior College.

As Lucas developed his image of Indy, he saw him as "more of a fortune hunter than a traditional scientist, but one who would only hunt for museums, so it had an air of legitimacy." Lucas envisioned

RAIDERS OF THE LOST ARK

Above a pit full of deadly snakes, Karen Allen clings to a statue for dear life as Indy, ankle-deep in vipers, prepares to rescue her (opposite).

Almost always the gentleman, Indy carries Allen across the snake pit as the crew follows the shot.

him as extremely intelligent, a college professor, although not a great one because he was more interested in adventures than teaching. "Originally, also, he was a playboy and lived this fast life in Manhattan," Lucas says. "He used his treasure hunting to fund his life-style. When we got on to that part of it, Steven and Harrison Ford both fought the idea. I kept pushing it and pushing it and it's still there; it's just not ever talked about.

"Especially in the first movie, Indy's driven by the significance of what he's going after, not the money. He's basically a mercenary, but it's the thrill of discovery that keeps him going. He loves archaeology and he loves discovering the truth about ancient civilizations and history."

From the start, as always, the cinematic delights that Lucas had in mind for *Raiders* were character-driven and story-driven. Lucas had first discussed the basic idea with another friend, Philip Kaufman, a Chicago-born filmmaker who had also abandoned Los Angeles for San Francisco and later made *The Right Stuff* and *The Unbearable Lightness of Being.* It was Kaufman who came up with the Ark of the Covenant as the engine for the story. He had heard about it from his doctor when he was eleven years old. Lucas hoped Kaufman would write and direct the film (he shares story credit with Lucas), but meantime Kaufman got a chance to do a Clint Eastwood film. Lucas put the story aside to do *Star Wars,* and there it rested until the conversation on the beach.

Lucas was, again, executive producer. He and Spielberg agreed on Frank Marshall, who had previously worked with Peter Bogdanovich for several years, as producer. Spielberg proposed Larry Kasdan, from whom he had bought a script called "Continental Divide," as the writer, and Lucas agreed. "They knew what they wanted," Kasdan says. "The character was going to be named for George's dog, Indiana, and George knew what Indy would wear and exactly what kind of movie it would be."

"What I learned on *Raiders,*" Lucas says, "is that you set the whole thing up. Get the script pretty much the way you want it. Then, if you hire the right person whom you agree with, you go with their vision. I let Steve direct it whatever way he wanted to direct it. But the truth is that we agreed completely on the vision. The only other person I'm that close to aesthetically is Ron Howard. With those two, we can almost finish each other's sentences. Francis and I are great friends, but creatively we see things very differently."

(NBC television interviewer Jim Brown once asked Lucas and Coppola what each would do if someone gave them $2 billion free and clear. Before Lucas could reply, Coppola laughed and said, "I'd

RAIDERS OF THE LOST ARK

Lucas (top), who wrote the basic stories for the Indiana Jones trilogy, was frequently on the *Raiders* locations but happy to leave the directing to Spielberg.

With Indy in the middle of the action (center), his race with the Nazis to find the Ark of the Covenant drives the story, and *Raiders* takes shape as an $18-million homage to the action films of the 30s.

Harrison Ford, wearing his familiar fedora, and Lucas take a break between shots (bottom).

RAIDERS OF THE LOST ARK

The film's dazzling special effects included a blue-screen shot in which a character becomes a ghastly ghost (left) after an illicit glimpse of the Ark.

But the most astonishing effect was the melting of a Nazi, commencing with the making of this lifelike model.

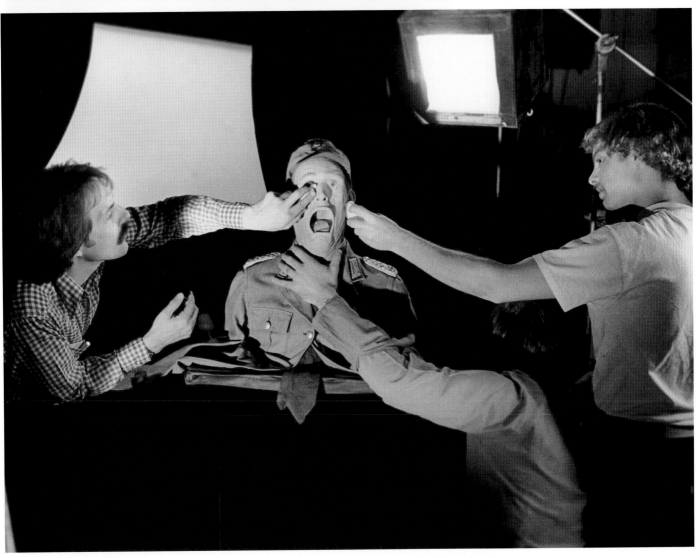

borrow another $2 billion and build a city." Lucas, gently mocking Coppola's free-spending ways, said later, "I'd invest a billion of it and use the other billion to build a town.")

Lucas had designed a small, handsome office building across Lankershim Boulevard from Universal in North Hollywood, and the preproduction meetings for *Raiders* took place there. "Larry [Kasdan], George, and Steven had a ball picking exciting moments they'd known as kids from the movies and wanted to see in a movie again," Marshall says. "I'd look at them and say, 'But where are we going to get a flying wing?' The practical side of it. But it was one of those times when you just come up with all the great toys and the wild ideas you can think of, and then you say, 'We can do it.' There was a great, positive atmosphere that George created. His motto was, 'We can do anything, and we can figure out how to do it for a price.' That was the challenge."

Michael Eisner, then at Paramount, read the first twenty pages of the script, Marshall remembers, "and said, 'That'll take the whole budget.' But George had enough clout already to say, 'We can do it, and here are the people involved.' And we did it. For $18 million. And it's still the most fun and the most rewarding producing experience I've ever had."

Luck was involved. The company learned that the submarine from the German film *Das Boot* was available in France in a cement submarine cavern, so it was written into the script.

Robert Watts, who had been production supervisor on *Star Wars,* took the same assignment on *Raiders.* He came to Hollywood in November 1979 to discuss logistics with Lucas and Spielberg. "Everyone was concerned. After all, we were shooting in seven countries on three continents. And if you can imagine moving a whole company from Tunisia to Hawaii! Yet we came in two weeks under schedule. George and Steven have a great relationship. It's a partnership made in heaven, sharing the creative endeavor. They're both responsible filmmakers. Steven loves directing, George doesn't. Steven takes in projects others have developed; George likes to develop all his own."

In a featurette on the shooting of *Raiders,* Harrison Ford is shown preparing for the first take of a sequence in which he is dragged behind a truck. As an assistant director comes over to tell him the shot is ready, Ford says, "Ah, well, here goes another useless learning experience." But Ford remarked recently that "Anybody who couldn't have fun doing that picture must have been dead for several years."

The special effects were spectacular, and never more so than when a boulder the size of an automobile rumbles down a tunnel, gaining on Indy as he runs, gasping and stumbling, trying to escape. The difference this time was that the effects were not creating reality within some future-tense galactic fantasy but within a cliff-hanging reality set in present time. As before, the trickeries were seamless.

And, as the phrase "star wars" was to be applied (to Lucas's discomfort) to the Strategic Defense Initiative, so "Indiana Jones" has gone into the language as identifying a type of daring adventurer. A Brazilian tycoon, for example, was described in a news story as "a real-life Indiana Jones." Lucas had, in tandem with Spielberg, once again made a permanent imprint on the world's imagination.

Scholarly observers noted, too, that once again in his basic story Lucas had drawn upon his interest in mythology, with its pittings of good vs. evil, and the hero battling villains in their joint quest for a token of power, in this case the Ark of the Covenant itself. The adventures, with their nonstop hairbreadth escapes, were enough to satisfy the appetites of any audience. But it could well be, as scholars insisted, that there was a deeper attraction, based on the subconscious appeal of those mythic elements. Then again, there was the slithery, squeal-inducing appeal of a pitful of six thousand deadly snakes.

Raiders of the Lost Ark quickly became the largest-grossing film of 1981, and one of the most popular films ever made.

RAIDERS OF THE LOST ARK

Going, going, gone—the camera cut imperceptibly from the living actor to the wax model, which melts before our disbelieving but appreciative eyes.

RAIDERS OF THE LOST ARK

On a *Raiders* location in Tozeur, Tunisia, Lucas joined Karen Allen, Steven Spielberg, and Harrison Ford.

The stagecoach is now a military truck, but Indy, trying to swing aboard from horseback, could as well have been in one of the Westerns whose spirit the film celebrates. The Ark of the Covenant is the prize in the truck.

From the ceiling Indy and Sallah (John Rhys-Davies) peer down into the Well of Souls (opposite) where the heroine will encounter the snake pit.

84

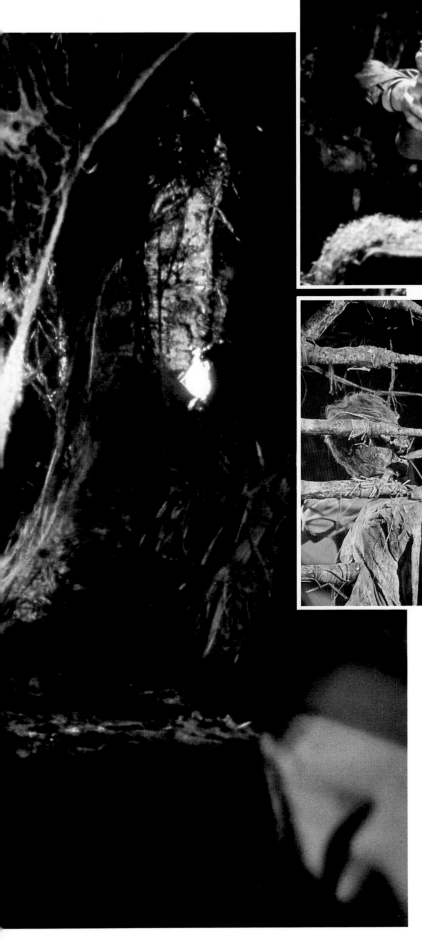

Indy gingerly lifts away a jeweled idol from its perch (top), quickly (but not quickly enough) replacing it with a bag of sand.

Spielberg checks a spear-pierced skeleton to be sure it will look sufficiently grisly.

In the best-remembered sequence from *Raiders,* Indy, having triggered a whole set of booby traps, is pursued down a tunnel by a giant boulder (opposite).

BODY HEAT [1981]

Just as Francis Coppola had used his influence to help Lucas make production deals for both *THX 1138* and *American Graffiti*, Lucas was now able, following his own success, to help other filmmakers get their work financed and made. In some cases he was, in effect, acting like a cosigner on a loan, although the promise was not of financial help but of creative backup in case the filmmaker ran into trouble. But Lucas's help was almost always as more than a guarantor. He gave counsel before, during, and after the shooting of a film, especially in the editing room, where he is most at home. He has, when necessary, taken a credit as executive producer, but occasionally he has been a silent partner.

Larry Kasdan, who had already written *The Empire Strikes Back* for Lucas and *Raiders of the Lost Ark* for Lucas and Spielberg, was in 1980 impatient to direct as well as write, and he had sold an original script called *Body Heat* to Alan Ladd, Jr.'s company at Warner Brothers. The agreement was that he could direct, on the proviso that he get a "name" director as sponsor and backup in case the production got into trouble.

Kasdan approached Lucas, who agreed to be an uncredited executive producer. "He thought this overseeing business was pretty ridiculous," Kasdan says. "He thought I was perfectly capable of directing the movie, and he didn't know what function an overseer served. But the tradition goes on, and now *I'm* doing it for somebody."

Lucas asked a fee that was more than Kasdan was being paid. But Lucas added that, if the film went over budget, Kasdan could apply the fee against the additional costs. "That was an extraordinarily generous thing to do," Kasdan says. "And he made it possible to make the film with no interference at all." Lucas later spent time in the editing room with Kasdan and his editor, Carol Littleton, and made what Kasdan says were very valuable suggestions.

Lucas felt it would be a huge mistake to have his name on the picture as executive producer. "There would have been a giant controversy about *me* making this picture," Lucas says, "and Larry would have gotten lost in the process. And it wasn't *me* making this picture, it was Larry."

The film, a homage to James M. Cain and the *noir* films of the 50s and 60s, was a sexy and powerful drama in which Kathleen Turner made her debut as a married woman who gets William Hurt to kill her husband. It was not the kind of material that has been associated with Lucas. But his support of Kasdan was an early indication of his eagerness to lend a hand to other filmmakers whose work he admired or whose promise he perceived. And the outstanding critical and commercial success of the movie suggested that Lucas's confidence in Kasdan was well placed.

BODY HEAT

Lucas and Lawrence Kasdan during production of an earlier Lucas film.

Kathleen Turner (opposite) is a sexy married *femme fatale* in Kasdan's first directing effort, on which Lucas was an uncredited executive producer.

TWICE UPON A TIME (1982)

Lucas, whose first student film at USC had been in a form of animation called "kinestasis," has always had an affection for the animator's art. In 1981 his Marin County neighbor and friend John Korty, who works in both live action and animation, told him about a feature film he wanted to do employing a special animation technique he had devised.

"I'd been working on a new kind of animation, which I called Lumage, from 'luminous images,'" Korty says. "The images were cut out and then lit from below, which gave them a special glow. I'd been aiming to do a feature in the technique, and I took the idea to George. He arranged an appointment for us with Laddie (Alan Ladd, Jr.) who agreed to finance the film."

It turned out to be a visually stunning and wittily sophisticated fantasy that bore about as much relation to traditional Disney cartoons as Salvador Dali's paintings did to Norman Rockwell's. An evil outfit called the Murkworks, led by a devilish character called Synonamess Botch, wants to replace the world's sweet dreams with nightmares, which are delivered as bomblike eardrops by a platoon of winged creatures resembling a cross between vultures and pterodactyls.

The wildly improbable good guys are led by Ralph, an all-purpose animal who can change from mole to lion in a trice, as the occasion demands, and who is partnered with Mumford, a top-hatted fellow, whose speech is a symphony of sound effects, very difficult to decipher. There is also a Fairy Godmother with a Bronx accent and a heroic-looking but singularly dense chap named Rod Rescueman. The sweet-dream world is presided over by an illiterate ruler who thus can't read the message warning him that the good guys are in trouble.

As the characters and their names indicate, *Twice Upon a Time* was a very hip enterprise in both form and content. The Lumage images are subtle and glowing, far more stylized than most feature animation. Conventional it isn't, and the verbal fun, like the punning in television's "Bullwinkle Show," is a bit too grown up for the smallest of the small fry.

"A lot of people from improvisational comedy were involved," Korty says. "Marshall Efron was the voice of the principal villain. Hamilton Camp was involved, and Paul Frees, who's been doing voices forever. Our mistake, I suppose, was to try to make a film that would appeal to everybody, all ages. There was a lot of slapstick in it, but it was much too sophisticated for four- and five-year-olds. We did our first sound mix at Lucasfilm up here in Marin, then finished in Los Angeles. George gave us a lot of great editorial feedback, mainly in the postproduction stages. But nobody knew quite how to sell it."

Adult audiences presume—wrongly, as in this case—that animated features are strictly for children. *Twice Upon a Time* played at a few theaters and did little business. But now, available on videocassette, it is being rediscovered as a richly imaginative, visually delightful, and decidedly offbeat animated treasure.

TWICE UPON A TIME

John Korty and Lucas discuss production notes.

The melding of background photographs and cartoony figures, as in this homage to Harold Lloyd's famous clock caper (opposite top), enhanced the film's surrealistic look.

Korty's perspectives and lacy constructions (opposite bottom) are brilliant but proved too sophisticated for the moppet trade.

RETURN OF THE JEDI (1983)

The three films of the *Star Wars* trilogy are obviously all of a piece, unified by the great conflict of the rebels vs. the Empire, by the three heroic central figures, and by Darth Vader as the principal villain. What is interesting is that within their obvious unities the films are subtly different from each other, with *The Empire Strikes Back* as the darkest of the three, resembling the second act of a three-act play, where the plot is building toward all the complications that must be triumphantly resolved in the last act.

To direct *Return of the Jedi,* Lucas turned to Richard Marquand, a young Englishman who had begun in commercials and then did a well-reviewed television series, "The Search for the Nile." His excellent feature film, a thriller called *Eye of the Needle,* was clearly a good recommendation for the Lucas project. Marquand later made another successful thriller, *Jagged Edge*; he died at only forty-nine in 1987.

Lawrence Kasdan, anxious to move on to directing, was preparing his first feature, but when Lucas asked him to write *Jedi* he agreed. "I liked George, and he was always under pressure—they were always starting these movies before they had scripts. So George and Richard Marquand and I had the same sort of sessions that we'd had with Kershner on *Empire.*"

The script was full of wonderful new creations, most notably the Ewoks, those furry, cuddly creatures, living teddy bears, so to speak, who dwelt in trees and who found such favor with audiences that they later became a spin-off hit in films for television. There was also that grossest of gangsters, Jabba the Hutt, and his Gamorrean Pig Guards.

Lucas did the second-unit photography on the Ewoks himself and made a useful discovery. He caught sight of one of the little people, Warwick Davis, an eleven-year-old, clowning between takes. Lucas, already thinking about *Willow,* realized that the film could be cast with little people, using Davis as the star. Lucas signed him to a contract, although *Willow* was still five years off. Lucas is, among his several characteristics, a long-term planner.

As production began in January 1982, its leads were six years older than when they had met to film *Star Wars:* Carrie Fisher, no longer a teenager but a mature woman; Mark Hamill, no longer on

RETURN OF THE JEDI

A road creature, resembling a giant mutant iguana and designed by Phil Tippett, lived near Jabba's palace in the background.

the verge of manhood but fully arrived; Harrison Ford, more than ever the world-weary odd man out.

Ford was seriously concerned that his Han Solo character was undermotivated this time. "I didn't think I was really involved in the story, so I had no idea of what to do with my character. We had tough discussions about that. Part of the brouhaha was that I thought my character should die. Since Han Solo had no momma and no poppa and wasn't going to get the girl anyway, he may as well die to give the whole thing some real emotional resonance. But George wouldn't agree to it." Lucas felt it would have been wrong in story terms, too downbeat for an upbeat film, but the debate did not impair a close and continuing friendship.

As before, the special effects were very special. Probably most unforgettably, there were the Speeder Bikes whizzing through the forest a few feet off the ground and representing a teenager's wildest dreams of excitement. The trickery worked so well that it is still hard to imagine that the Speeder Bike doesn't really exist and has simply not yet reached the consumer market.

Warren Franklin remembers, with a shake of the head, that the script simply said, "They jump on their Speeder Bikes and take off at 120 miles an hour through the forest." It was up to the special-effects teams to make it work. "The challenge just dropped into our laps," Franklin says. "At first we planned to build a miniature forest, but we realized it would have to be *huge*. Dennis Muren, one of the special-effects supervisors, finally hit on the idea of just going out into the redwoods. We actually took a road and painted it green and dressed it and then walked a camera along it, with a guide wire to keep the camera at the right angle. Then we simply came back to ILM and put the actors in it. It was a lot of fun."

"People occasionally say I'm the new Walt Disney," Lucas has said. "But I'm not really the new Walt Disney at all. Yet one thing occurred to me when Jim Henson died. People said he was the new Walt Disney, too. But the truth is that what Walt did for animation Jim did for puppetry and I've done for special effects. I took something that was not very well regarded, a kind of esoteric, technical-cult enthusiasm, and recognized it for the art it is and gave it a showcase where people could really see and appreciate the artistry."

Says Kasdan, "George understood that you could integrate the effects into the story so that they formed part of the story in a way that people had never really tried before. The story was going on in the foreground, but now through the window of the ship amazing effects were taking place."

The tone of the trilogy is very much Lucas, Kasdan feels,

Ever in trouble of one kind or another, Han Solo and
Luke Skywalker are trapped by Ewoks brandishing
sharp sticks. On further acquaintance, the Ewoks turned
out to be friends, not foes.

RETURN OF THE JEDI

In a highly charged moment, the Emperor, formerly Senator Palpatine, descends a staircase on the Death Star, attempting to destroy Luke.

A composite photograph (opposite) brought together all the *Star Wars* spacecrafts, the Empire's Tie fighters (above the Millennium Falcon), the rebels' X-wings (below center), and the Death Star.

essentially cheerful and ebullient. "Yet there is this other, this dark side." Paradoxically, Kasdan found that Lucas—who has made such brilliant use of technology— has a deeply rooted belief that technology is dangerous. "He believes that a larger mechanical force is vulnerable to a natural force. You can look at *Jedi* and see the Vietnam War there. You can see the Ewok guerrillas hiding in the jungles, taking on this improper force of mechanized bullies— and winning."

Jedi was released May 25, 1983, six years to the day after *Star Wars.* The critics seemed astonished that Lucas had sustained his vision—and his gift for surprise—through not one but two sequels. The film was another large commercial success. And now the scholars were reading new significances into the films Lucas and his collaborators had wrought.

One author argued that C-3PO and R2-D2 demonstrated the philosopher Henri Bergson's notion of the comedy inherent in the conflict of man vs. machine—including the double reversal of a machine acting like a man acting like a machine. Another author saw in Luke Skywalker an exemplar of the American Adam, the prototypical American represented by real and fictional figures as various as Thoreau and Captain Ahab.

In a 1983 paper, "The Myth and Magic of *Star Wars,*" Maurice Phipps said that the popularity of the films might be explained not simply by the special effects and the adventures but by the connections the films made with the collective and personal unconscious of the viewers. The myths that touch Lucas appear to touch us all.

RETURN OF THE JEDI

R2-D2 and C-3PO, loyal and imperiled as usual, struggle through thick vegetation of the Forest of Endor (top).

Near the end of the film, Luke removes the black helmet and confirms the real identity of the dying Darth Vader.

Leia and Solo (opposite) hold off the enemy while trying to get into the Imperial bunker on the Moon of Endor.

INDIANA JONES AND THE TEMPLE OF DOOM (1984)

Raiders of the Lost Ark had roamed all over the map for its cliff-hanging thrills. *Indiana Jones and the Temple of Doom* was quite different. It was largely concentrated in one place, the Temple of Doom itself, with its pitiable child laborers and its human sacrifices, involving the extraction of a still-beating heart, and a fiery furnace into which sacrificial victims (or unlucky intruders) were lowered. It was a tougher, more frightening film by far.

Lucas's old friends Willard Huyck and Gloria Katz, who had written the final version of *American Graffiti,* were hired to do the script from his story. There was some question whether Spielberg would want to direct the sequel; generally, Hollywood directors prefer not to do the follow-ups to their hits. "I'm afraid we might lose him, so you guys better get this done fast," Huyck says Lucas warned them. The script pleased Spielberg, and he overcame his reluctance. "Steven was amazed," Huyck adds. "He couldn't get out of it because we did it so fast."

Lucas was executive producer, along with Frank Marshall from Spielberg's team. Robert Watts was the producer.

In story conferences the question was how dark was the movie going to be. "George wanted it to be really scary," Huyck says. "Steve was leery at first, but then he got into it; and when Steve does something, he does it to the nth degree. Writing those movies you work out from the action sequences. You have this great action, then you have to find a story to put it in."

The critic Roger Ebert called the film's theme "The Impregnable Fortress Impregnated." He added that a man was likely to come away with his forearm bruised where his date had squeezed it, screaming, during the moments of high excitement.

ILM outdid itself with two final sequences. There is the great escape, as Indy, the heroine (Kate Capshaw), and Short Round (Ke Huy Quan) flee the Temple of Doom aboard an ore car. As the car careens along rickety rails deep in the mine, ILM mixed live action and miniatures so expertly that it is impossible to tell where the live action begins and the miniatures leave off.

The final action sequence, on a swaying rope bridge across a rocky gorge that looks deeper than the Grand Canyon, is another nail-biting sequence, the illusion so perfect that it is hard to believe the actors were not in peril. As *The Empire Strikes Back* had confounded the usual expectations by being as thrilling and inventive as *Star Wars, Indiana Jones and the Temple of Doom* was received as the equal of the original, although it was to be the heaviest of the trilogy—really scary, as Lucas intended.

THE TEMPLE OF DOOM

As the Indiana Jones trilogy continued, Harrison Ford, a minor player in *American Graffiti*, became a major Hollywood star, his Indy characterization ever more worldly wise and sardonic (top).

Indy and his new leading lady, Kate Capshaw, discover something unpleasant at the Club Obi-Wan (a jokey reference to the *Star Wars* trilogy).

Indy's sidekick, Short Round, thrusts a burning torch at one of the villainous Mola Ram's guards (opposite) and helps Indy escape from the underground Temple.

THE TEMPLE OF DOOM

Reunited on location in Sri Lanka, Lucas and Harrison Ford posed with a majestically tusked local elephant (above).

Having escaped from one peril, Indy and Short Round (Ke Huy Kwan) find themselves in another, bouncing down a river white with rapids. The wetness is real enough as they wait for Spielberg to call, "Action."

THE TEMPLE OF DOOM

A chilling chilled dessert, monkey brains on the half-skull, concludes a meal at the Pankot Palace and horrifies Kate Capshaw, as well it might. The second Indy film was the blackest of the three.

At the Royal Premiere in London of *Temple of Doom* on June 11, 1984, Lucas attended with Capshaw, Spielberg, Kathy Kennedy, and Frank Marshall (opposite top).

Near the end of the *Temple of Doom* shooting, Spielberg and Lucas both looked exhausted.

THE TEMPLE OF DOOM

The mine-tunnel escape, a high point of the film, had Indy and Short Round riding an out-of-control ore car (above).

A slave camera, mounted on the front of the ore car, took close-ups of the passengers. Live-action and miniature photography were indistinguishably intercut.

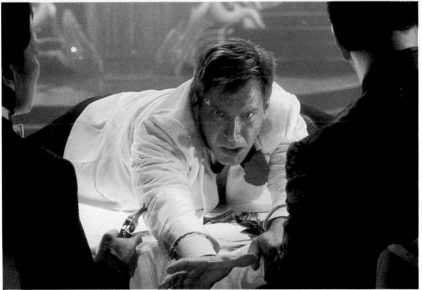

THE TEMPLE OF DOOM

In the infamous Club Obi-Wan (above), Indy realizes he's been poisoned and has only seconds to find the antidote. As the writers in the series—Willard Huyck and Gloria Katz in this case—have all found, the trick is to invent perils that, despite everything, Indy can survive.

Gasping for breath, Indy fights his way toward the antidote. The pleasure of the series is that the action somehow is able to be dramatic and suspenseful, but also funny rather than deeply worrying.

THE EWOK ADVENTURES (1984–1985)

After the success of the *Star Wars* films and the ratings the films earned when broadcast, it was inevitable that television would find something for Lucasfilm to do directly for the small screen.

That first something proved to be the Ewoks, the lovable, furry, tree-dwelling creatures from *Return of the Jedi*. Lucas created two Ewok adventures, each of which appeared as "The ABC Sunday Night Movie," the first in November 1984, the second a year later. Both were intriguing mixtures of future and past, star cruisers and forest creatures, space guns and monsters and a wicked queen.

The first film was *The Ewok Adventure: Caravan of Courage,* with a script by Bob Carrau. To direct it, Lucas recruited his Marin County neighbor and friend John Korty. Thomas G. Smith was producer, and the film was designed by Joe Johnston, who began as a storyboard artist on *Star Wars* and has subsequently directed *Honey, I Shrunk the Kids* and *The Rocketeer*.

A family's star cruiser crashes in Ewok country on the forest moon of Endor. The parents go off to seek help. When they don't return, their two children take off on their own, having narrow escapes from strange beasts until they fall into the friendly hands of the Ewoks, led by Wicket (Warwick Davis, who was in *Return of the Jedi* and later starred in the title role in *Willow*). Eric Walker and Aubree Miller played the brother and sister, Fionnula Flanagan and Guy Boyd the parents, with Burl Ives as the narrator.

A second film, *Ewoks: The Battle for Endor,* was broadcast in November 1985, written from Lucas's story and directed by the brother team of Jim and Ken Wheat, with Lucas again as executive producer. Ugly invaders led by a giant, King Terak, attack an Ewok village, killing the parents and the brother of the girl (Aubree Miller) from the first film. She and Wicket escape, find shelter with a crusty hermit (Wilford Brimley), and end up in the clutches of a wicked witch, Charal, played quite deliciously by Sian Phillips. ILM contributed some splendid special effects, of a quality rare in television, to both films. The critics agreed they were superior television fare. Both were shown theatrically abroad.

The success of *Caravan of Courage* led to a further spin-off, half-hour animated adventure series, one featuring the Ewoks and one the Droids. "Ewoks and Droids Adventure Hour" ran on ABC in the fall of 1985. The Droid half-hour featured Anthony Daniels, who was C-3PO in the *Star Wars* films, as the voice of the Golden Robot. In 1986, "Ewoks" returned for a second season. The cartoons were Nelvana Productions for Lucasfilm Ltd., "Based on characters created by George Lucas."

THE EWOK ADVENTURES

John Korty (opposite), who directed *Caravan of Courage,* knelt to talk with its heroine, Aubree Miller, and Warwick Davis, one of the little people who played the Ewoks.

The prisoner of a wicked king, Aubree Miller (below) faces death if she doesn't reveal her family's magic.

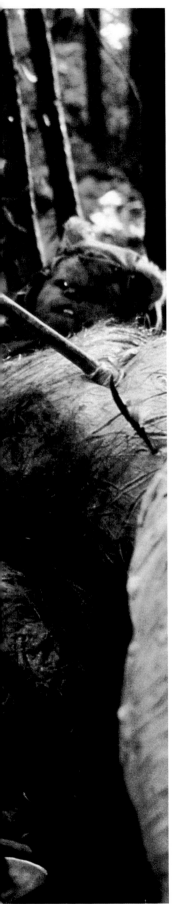

Trapped in dangerous rapids in the "Haunted Village" episode of the animated Ewok series, Princess Kneesa poles madly to save Latara (top).

Wicket the Ewok travels in high style, hang-gliding over a forest under a threatening sky in the "Asha" episode.

Eric Walker is caught in the battle between a ruthless giant and the kindly Ewoks (opposite).

RETURN TO OZ [1985]

Lucas's USC classmate Walter Murch, who had coauthored the first treatment for the student-film version of "THX 1138," had gone on to his own career as an editor. In 1984 he was making his debut as a director with *Return to Oz,* which he had also coauthored. It was a sequel to *The Wizard of Oz* and starred Fairuza Balk as the new Dorothy, who escapes from a very nasty asylum in Kansas and, on reaching Oz again, finds it being run by a set of evil characters led by the Nome King. The adults in view included Jean Marsh from television's "Upstairs Downstairs," who was later to play Queen Bavmorda in *Willow,* and the English stage actor Nicol Williamson.

The film, which was being shot in London, ran into cost and production problems and Murch asked Lucas if he would come over and take a look. Lucas quickly agreed and began commuting between San Francisco and London. He asked for his expenses only, no salary, and he wanted to take no credit.

"I told Walter I didn't want to be officially involved because *Return to Oz* would then be viewed as *my* picture, not his. The critics came crashing down on the picture anyway, but they didn't come down nearly as hard as they would have if my name had been on it." As it is, the film simply has a credit at the end thanking Lucas and Robert Watts, the veteran production manager who also consulted on the film.

There are some fine moments in the film, including some clay animation by Will Vinton. But the new make-believe was evidently too gloomy for the lovers of the original trip to Oz.

MISHIMA [1985]

As part of their continuing interest in encouraging other young filmmakers, Lucas and Coppola in 1984 became joint executive producers of *Mishima,* by Paul Schrader, a feisty and adventurous writer-filmmaker they both knew and admired.

Schrader, who had begun as a film journalist and critic while awaiting his chance to write and direct scripts, had made his directing debut with *Blue Collar,* a tense and atmospheric drama about auto factory workers.

The ambitiously conceived *Mishima,* cowritten by Schrader and his brother Leonard, was partly a biography (in black-and-white segments) of the controversial Japanese author Yukio Mishima, who had ended his life with a ceremonial public suicide in 1970. Interspersed with the biography were dramatized scenes, in brilliant color, from his highly symbolic, stylized, and intensely personal novels, in which Mishima celebrated both the quest for absolute beauty and the glories of Japan's chivalrous warrior past, including the ideal of an honorable death sustained in battle.

Lucas persuaded Terry Semel of Warner Brothers to finance half of the film, and he read and commented on the script and visited the production while Schrader was shooting in Japan. The film was released by Warners, as a coproduction of Zoetrope Studios, Lucasfilm Ltd., and Filmlink International (Tokyo).

Mishima, an artistic triumph, has acquired a cult following, but Mishima's life and work were so little known in the United States that the film played to relatively small audiences.

THE RETURN TO OZ

Fairuza Balk, the later Dorothy who returns to a much-changed Oz, listens to director Walter Murch.

MISHIMA

Actor Ken Ogato (opposite) played the Japanese author Yukio Mishima in Paul Schrader's ambitious film about the man who died in a ceremonial public suicide.

MISHIMA

**Paul Schrader's film intermixes three elements: visually
amazing interpretations of Mishima's fiction (opposite top),
black-and-white biographical scenes (opposite center),
and in color, the events of his final day (above), which
serve as the framework for the film. Mishima, who thought
of himself as a latter-day samurai, committed hara-kiri.**

**Writer-director Schrader (at left, opposite bottom) and
John Bailey, who did the film's exquisite cinematography,
confer with Lucas during production.**

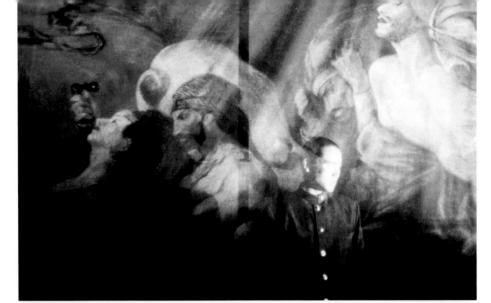

LATINO

Before a battle scene Haskell Wexler lectures his actors (right) on location in Nicaragua, which was doubling for Honduras, where the training of the Contras by U.S. forces was supposed to have taken place.

Wexler, an Oscar-winning cinematographer who did much of the shooting on *American Graffiti*, created memorable images in his film, as in this dusty battle between the Contras and the Sandinistas.

LATINO (1986)

"On the one hand I'm doing these huge productions and at the same time I'm helping on these little productions, for my friends," Lucas has said. "They're all interesting movies, movies that I cared about and wanted to see made one way or another. Some of them were small failures, some of them were huge failures, and some were extremely nice movies. But in most of the interviews with me, and even within the company, they're passed right over, as though they never existed. But those movies may be closer to what I am than *Star Wars*."

The fine cinematographer Haskell Wexler, a friend since Lucas's days at USC, had later been an invaluable consultant on the problems of night shooting on *American Graffiti*. He won an Academy Award for his photography on *Who's Afraid of Virginia Woolf?* in 1966 and his first feature as a director, *Medium Cool*, remains one of the best films about the political turmoil of the 60s.

Always politically concerned, Wexler in 1984 wanted to do *Latino,* an angry and, indeed, polemical film about the U. S. involvement in Central America, and Nicaragua specifically. Lucas, who appreciates Wexler's fierce dedication, read and advised on the script and later on the editing, and lent his backing, which helped Wexler obtain a distribution deal with Cinecom.

Actually filmed in Nicaragua, *Latino* starred Robert Beltran as a Chicano who had been a Green Beret in Vietnam and was now leading the Contras against the Sandinistas.

Like *Medium Cool, Latino* has a documentary feeling, conveying a strong sense of the realities of the civil strife within Nicaragua. But, like other politically committed films, it did not appeal to audiences conditioned to less urgent material.

THE GREAT HEEP (1986)

Ben Burtt, the sound designer who developed the eerie and original sound effects for *Star Wars* and subsequent Lucas films, turned his hand to writing and created the script for *The Great Heep,* an hour-long animated special that aired on ABC in 1986.

Lucas's droll Droid inventions from *Star Wars,* Artoo-Detoo (R2-D2) and See-Threepio (C-3PO), set off to join a new master, the explorer Mungo Baobab on the planet Biitu, only to find Mungo and the planet in the hands of a huge and very evil Droid called the Great Heep. R2-D2 falls in love with a female Droid called KT-10, and C-3PO joins up with a boy named Fidge and his pet, Chubb. Together they tackled the Heep.

Several Lucas veterans teamed up with the Canadian animation firm Nelvana Ltd. to make *The Great Heep.* Anthony Daniels was again the voice of C-3PO, and the Heep was designed by Joe Johnston, who also designed the made-for-TV Ewok adventures. Miki Herman, executive producer on the special, had been unit production manager on *Return of the Jedi* and was executive producer on the first season of ABC's "The Ewoks and Droids Adventure Hour."

Burtt subsequently directed the documentary *Blue Planet,* in the large-screen IMAX format.

THE GREAT HEEP

Mungo Baobab, the new master of R2-D2 and C-3PO, rides a strange new beast called a Rock Hopper and is pursued by the evil giant Droid, the Great Heep.

LABYRINTH (1986)

Like almost everyone else on earth, Lucas was a great admirer of Jim Henson, the creator of the Muppets. Henson's vision of his art, sophisticated and fantastical but embodying timeless values of friendship, loyalty, compassion, and optimism, was close to Lucas's' own. Kermit and Miss Piggy, no less than the curmudgeonly old gents in the theater box and Bert and Ernie, were creatures after Lucas's heart.

Henson's continuing quest for new creative ventures also appealed to Lucas. When Henson proposed that Lucasfilm and his Henson Associates coproduce a non-Muppets film called *Labyrinth,* Lucas was eager to participate.

The film is a kind of far-out variation on *Alice in Wonderland,* written by Terry Jones of the Monty Python crew and touched by the antic spirit of that group. A rather spoiled teenager (Jennifer Connelly), sentenced to baby-sit her very young brother while the parents go out for the evening, makes a mumbo-jumbo wish that he would disappear. So he does—kidnapped by David Bowie as King of the Goblins. To retrieve him, the girl will have to track him through the Labyrinth, which is all the scary Halloween houses of the world rolled into one, a place of mazelike passages, doors that appear and disappear magically, of trapdoors and cobwebby caves, scary noises and bizarre creatures, one or two of whom actually turn out to be friendly. Even the unfriendly creatures are, like the inhabitants of Alice's Wonderland, strange rather than horrifying. And, in the best fairy-tale tradition, *Labyrinth* is full of good, sensible morals, like "Don't make wishes you don't really mean," and "Be patient with your kid brother; he can't help it."

LABYRINTH

Jim Henson (above), creator of the Muppets, dreamed up a new set of characters for his "Alice in Wonderland"–like fantasy.

A meeting of imaginations: Jim Henson, creator of the Muppets, and Lucas confer during the making of Henson's film.

As her punishment, Jennifer Connelly, the baby-sitter who ignores her sleeping brother, finds herself in a nightmarish and weirdly populated maze (opposite).

LABYRINTH

Pop star David Bowie (top) is the King of the Goblins, who controls the teenager's fate.

All dressed up as Bowie's consort in a fantasy within the fantasy, the teenager realizes what a mess she's in.

Despite his fearsome appearance, the mournful giant Ludo turns out to be a sympathetic friend, and in that neighborhood the teenager could use one (opposite).

HOWARD THE DUCK (1986)

While Lucas was working with his friends Willard Huyck and Gloria Katz on the script of "Radioland Murders" (one of his projects that percolated for more than a dozen years), he mentioned in passing how much he enjoyed the "Howard the Duck" comic books. He passed along some copies to the Huycks.

"George said, 'I think you guys would really like this, because you have a weird sense of humor,'" Huyck says. "Years went by. We could never get the rights. Eventually they became available and we called George and said, 'Listen. We can do Howard.'"

Lucas had reservations when Universal asked him to sponsor the film (as he had sponsored Kasdan's *Body Heat*) because it was already looking like an expensive and tricky project. But to help the Huycks, with whom he had written the original treatment and then the final script of *American Graffiti*, Lucas agreed. He worried about using a man in a duck suit in lieu of a duck animated like the Toons in *Who Framed Roger Rabbit*. The Huycks liked the idea of a smaller duck, perhaps Muppet-like. "But we could never figure out how to build the stupid thing," Huyck says.

Lucas worried too, that introducing a monster late in the film could change the nature of the comedy. "But the die had been pretty much cast when I got involved," Lucas says, "so I endeavored to help Bill bring his version to the screen." Gloria Katz says, "Originally we were going to do it much differently, but that wasn't the way Universal wanted to do it. We wanted to do it in a sort of *film noir* way, as a smaller, realistic story." Huyck adds, "Actually, the story was much more like *Roger Rabbit*. George said the same thing. He said, 'It would be great to do it and not explain, just have Howard be a detective.'"

Universal had noted the success of *Ghostbusters*, a comedy-fantasy, and was eager to leap on that particular bandwagon. "So it grew bigger and bigger," says Katz, "and it got all out of whack, to say the least."

Lucas fought to help Huyck keep the costs down, but the film ended up 20 percent over budget. "And the rest is history," Katz says with a sigh.

The reviews were almost uniformly terrible. Lucas is convinced that the fact his name was on *Howard the Duck* as executive producer made the reviews even harsher than they might otherwise have been. "If I hadn't been identified with the project, the reviews might have been a little gentler, at least," Lucas says.

"It always looked like a midget in a duck suit. You couldn't get around it," Huyck says. Lucas, as well as Huyck and Katz, have watched with amusement the later success of *Teenage Mutant Ninja Turtles*, which contains unmistakable human beings in turtle suits. "I guess we chose the wrong pond critter," Lucas says philosophically.

HOWARD THE DUCK

Howard the Duck, eager to audition but not greatly optimistic, waits in a hotel corridor (opposite).

Howard's specialized reading matter includes "Rolling Egg" and "Playduck."

HOWARD THE DUCK

Backstage at a rock concert (right), Howard talks with Tim Robbins as a young scientist and Lea Thompson, a rock singer in a group called Cherry Bomb.

Jeffrey Jones is Dr. Jennings (below), a scientist whose body is taken over by an evil alien called The Dark Overlord, with dreadful consequences for Jennings.

Performing at last, Howard takes the stage with Lea Thompson and her group and enjoys a moment of triumph.

HOWARD THE DUCK

Monstrous things happen to the luckless Dr. Jennings as
the evil alien inside him, capable of turning into
anything, turns into a geneticist's nightmare (above).

Howard at the controls of an Ultralight airplane lifts Tim
Robbins off the hood of a car, and they head on toward
the conclusion of the plot.

CAPTAIN EO (1986)

In 1985 Disney approached Lucas to create a super-duper film to play in a brand-new venue called the Magic Eye Theater that was being built at both Disneyland in Anaheim, California and Disney's Epcot Center in Orlando, Florida. (It also became part of the Disney World in Tokyo, which opened later.)

Lucas wrote the script for *Captain EO* himself and engaged his old friend Francis Coppola to direct it, with the singing, dancing, and song-writing star Michael Jackson, then at the peak of his phenomenal popularity, as the principal star. John Napier (who designed *Cats*) did the sets, Geoffrey Kirkland was the art director, Jeffrey Hornaday (*A Chorus Line*) was the choreographer, and Vittorio Storaro (*Apocalypse Now*) was the photographic consultant.

Jackson plays the captain of a spaceship that lands in an alien world run by an evil queen, played by Anjelica Huston. Jackson's crew includes oddball characters—animals and robots, with names like Fuzzball, Major Domo, and Hooter. Shot in 3-D and featuring animation by Disney and special effects by ILM, the film cost $10 million, which, for 17 minutes running time, makes it one of the most expensive films, per minute, ever made. The Jackson crew uses song and dance (including two new Jackson songs) to convince the aliens that peace is better.

It was an offbeat assignment for Lucas, and it reflected a sharp awareness within the industry of his exceptional gift for creating entertainment events with appeal to a very wide audience.

Captain EO (the name is based on the Greek word for "dawn") opened simultaneously at the theme parks in California and Florida and has been one of the most popular attractions in both locations ever since.

POWAQQATSI (1988)

Lucas had been impressed by the strikingly innovative film *Koyaanisqatsi*, by a filmmaker named Godfrey Reggio, which appeared in 1983. Francis Coppola had been the executive producer.

The title is a Hopi Indian word that has several interpretations, including "life in turmoil," "life out of balance," and "a condition of life that demands another way of living." With no narrative but with a minimalist score by the well-known composer Philip Glass, *Koyaanisqatsi* uses stop-motion photography (which speeds up the images crossing the screen) to contrast the beauty of natural landscapes with the horrors of industrial landscapes. It was a film of extremes—nature at its most majestic, man at his most despoiling. It was also the kind of innovative, expressive, and experimental film that Lucas himself had done in his student days, the style not unlike that of "6.18.67."

Koyaanisqatsi was undeniably striking, although a few critics attacked its either/or simplicity as being unrealistic in the modern world.

When Reggio proposed to do a sequel to *Koyaanisqatsi*, called *Powaqqatsi*, as the second leg of what was projected as a trilogy, Coppola had trouble finding financial backing, despite the first film's generally positive reception. Lucas stepped in and used his influence to help Reggio get distribution through Cannon Films.

Powaqqatsi extends Reggio's alarmed vision of the man-made future to the Third World, where the same kind of wordless but eloquent images record the exploitation of the resources of underdeveloped countries by the developed nations. Shot in ten countries from Peru to France, *Powaqqatsi* looks at the faces of the poor, often in the harsh sunlight that seems symbolic of harsh lives. Reggio and his cameramen, Graham Berry and Leonidas Zourdoumis, make use of aerial photography, telephoto lenses, optical effects, and again, stop-motion work, to create a kind of angry surrealism. Philip Glass was again the composer of the disturbing musical score. *Powaqqatsi*, another Hopi word, means, roughly, "life lived at the expense of others" or a "life of exploitation." Ironically, camera technology was brilliantly employed to record the negative impact on lives that modern technology can have.

CAPTAIN EO

Coppola and Lucas posed with Michael Jackson, the star of the multimillion-dollar 3-D film Lucas produced and Coppola directed for Disney (opposite).

POWAQQATSI

Symbolizing his film's theme of the inequitable distribution of the fruits of technological progress, Godfrey Reggio showed a jet passing over a vast warrenlike housing estate and its drying laundry (right).

WILLOW (1988)

George Lucas's fascination with mythology as the fountainhead of great drama runs through most of the films he has had a hand in. But the purest and most primal expression of his love of mythology is undoubtedly *Willow.*

It is a magical tale, set in a medieval past, of the finding of an infant by a colony of little people called the Nelwyns. In a gender reversal of the story of Moses hidden in the bulrushes, the baby, Elora Danan, has been hidden by her nurse because the wicked Queen Bavmorda has ordered the destruction of all female babies. It has been foretold that one of the infants will be her successor. The baby of the prophecy is indeed Elora. Willow, the 3-foot-high hero who finds her, sets out to return the infant to her rightful destiny.

Willow was played by Warwick Davis, whom Lucas met when he was cast as one of the Ewoks in *Return of the Jedi* and whose charm, agility, and intelligence persuaded Lucas that *Willow* could indeed be cast with little people.

Along the way, Willow recruits a full-size rogue, Madmartigan (Val Kilmer), a sort of Han Solo of the forests, who will eventually confront the evil queen and her protective two-headed dragon (one of ILM's proudest achievements). There is also a Vader-like figure called General Kael.

Many of the story elements—the child of destiny, the good caretakers, the skeptical elders, the monster to be vanquished, the dark castle where a malevolent ruler terrorizes all in sight—have, in various permutations, been the stuff of folklore and mythology for centuries.

Lucas's first and only choice to direct the film, which had been scripted by Bob Dolman from the Lucas story, was Ron Howard. Howard, an eighteen-year-old when Lucas first cast him in *American Graffiti,* was now a director with three successful films (including *Splash*) under his belt. "I wanted somebody with a sense of humor and somebody who would be good with the human side of this," Lucas says. "It's so easy to get overwhelmed with the effects and the logistics."

Dennis Muren, whose love of special effects began in childhood and who had joined Lucas as a motion-control camera operator on *Star Wars,* was a special-effects supervisor on *Willow.* The film was, he remembers, "an awful lot of work under the most difficult possible conditions, which is doing effects work in daylight instead of dark or nighttime. It's three times harder. There was this two-headed dragon at the end, and there were these Brownies that had

to be all over the place." (The Brownies, Rool and Franjean, were mischief makers 9 inches tall, played by Kevin Pollak and Rick Overton, who, in some amazing visual effects, are involved with both the larger little people and the full-size actors.)

The visual astonishments further included a goat who evolves through the forms of several other animals, before our very eyes, before she is revealed as a kindly sorceress named Raziel (Patricia Hayes), who is just emerging from a curse imposed by Queen Bavmorda (who was played to the hilt by Jean Marsh). "George," Muren recalls, "said he didn't care what happened in between, but he knew the scene started with a goat and ended up with a woman." Muren and *his* wizards turned to computer-generated images to bring off the seemingly miraculous transformations.

The casting of Warwick Davis and the other little people, a bold departure since they are not merely incidental but are central to the plot, lends *Willow* a particular and affecting charm. As Sheila Benson wrote in the *Los Angeles Times, Willow* "leaves a friendly glow and a sense of a magical world lovingly evoked."

WILLOW

The sword-brandishing General Kael (an unusual name but not unknown to filmmakers) is a vivid and menacing figure (opposite) in Lucas's celebration of the power of myth.

Patricia Hayes as the sorceress Raziel and Warwick Davis as Willow prepare to enter the evil Queen Bavmorda's castle and rescue the child of destiny.

WILLOW

Caged by Queen Bavmorda's troops, Val Kilmer as Madmartigan (above) implores Gavan O'Herlihy as Airk to free him so they can join forces to fight the queen.

At the castle where Bavmorda dwells, Kilmer and Joanne Whalley as Sorsha ponder their next move (opposite top).

Warwick Davis was the title figure, and Billy Barty played The High Aldwin (as in "Old One").

WILLOW

Chris Evans (top), an artist at ILM, works on a meticulous matte painting that will become the background for one of the film's sweeping pastoral scenes.

In this composite image from the film, Evans's painting merges undetectably with the stream-cut landscape in the foreground.

A host of the youngsters and little people who portrayed the Nelwyns cluster around director Ron Howard and Lucas (opposite).

WILLOW

Jean Marsh (top), famous for her role in "Upstairs Downstairs," becomes the wicked Queen Bavmorda, leaving her company manners behind.

Warwick Davis as Willow, with his wife, carries the infant girl he has found hidden beside a stream near the Nelwyns' village.

Surrounded by troops (opposite), Madmartigan, Sorsha, and Willow face an uncertain future.

WILLOW

Mixing the traditions of myth and Hollywood swashbuckling, Val Kilmer swings a mean sword (top) in a duel with one of the queen's henchmen.

The Eborsisk, a toothy two-headed monster created at ILM, guards the entrance to an abandoned castle.

Director Ron Howard (opposite), a long way from the lovesick teenager in *American Graffiti*, goes over the script with the veteran actor Billy Barty on location in England.

TUCKER: THE MAN AND HIS DREAM (1988)

Preston Tucker was a figure in American history who had a double appeal for both Lucas and Francis Coppola. Like both of them, Tucker was a maverick. At the end of World War II he undertook a daring gamble, to defy the Big Three American automakers, Ford, Chrysler, and General Motors, and design and manufacture a car of his own. He may even have thought of it not as an act of defiance but only as a dream of making a better car than the Big Three were turning out.

To a pair of mavericks who had elected to try making films outside Hollywood, Tucker was a kinsman. To Coppola, with his fascination with new technology, and to Lucas, with his lifelong love of cars, Tucker, with his Tucker automobile, was a hugely attractive figure.

Tucker's bold try was in the end unsuccessful, largely because of the political harassment instigated on behalf of the Big Three. But he had introduced several innovations, among them seat belts and independent four-wheel suspension, that would influence car design and construction long after the last of the fifty Tucker automobiles had rolled off the hand-tooled assembly line.

Lucas personally put up the money so Coppola could begin preproduction work on *Tucker,* then Paramount agreed to become the principal backer and the distributor of the film. *Tucker* became a Lucasfilm Ltd./Zoetrope Studios production, with Lucas as executive producer, Fred Roos and Fred Fuchs as producers, and with Coppola directing a script by David Seidler and Arnold Schulman. *Willow* was already in production in England, and Lucas commuted between the U.K. and Marin County to work on the development of *Tucker.*

Jeff Bridges made a charismatic Tucker, and his father, Lloyd, gave a chilling cameo performance as the real-life Michigan senator who inspired the government's assaults on Tucker (or its defense of the Big Three, depending on your point of view). Martin Landau won an Academy Award nomination for his portrayal of Tucker's loyal financial advisor.

In the end, defeated, Tucker makes some strong and prophetic

TUCKER

The 48th Tucker car rolls off the assembly line in Ypsilanti, Michigan, with Frederic Forest (left) and Christian Slater (in baseball cap), as Tucker's son, helping affix the front bumper.

warnings about the fate of a society that fails to encourage its mavericks and, in fact, persecutes them rather than unsettle a complacent establishment. "You'll one day be buying your cars from the Japanese," he warns.

Like Coppola (who owns two of them), Lucas acquired one of the Tucker cars (of which many are still running and exciting to see some forty years after they were made).

For reasons that are not really clear, especially in light of the American fascination with cars, *Tucker* was not a popular success. The likeliest explanation is that, although the script gave Tucker a notable—and historically accurate—courtroom triumph, the dream collapsed and the car died. The film's upbeat conclusion could not disguise reality's downbeat ending.

TUCKER

Jeff Bridges as the charismatic Preston Tucker (top) delivers his shirt-sleeved pitch in a boardroom.

Coppola's split-screen technique put Martin Landau as Tucker's finance man and Tucker in the same frame.

Fighting for the life of his automobile, Tucker makes an impassioned plea to a jury in Washington, D.C.

Joan Allen as Tucker's wife, Vera, makes her own pitch
for her husband in the boardroom.

TUCKER

A meeting of mavericks (top): Tucker and a sympathetic Howard Hughes (played by Dean Stockwell) talk beneath Hughes's own ambitious but doomed project, the Spruce Goose.

Vindicated by the jury, Tucker waves to the crowd during a triumphant motorcade around the courthouse.

TUCKER

Showing off the sketch of the prototype car (top), Tucker tries to fire up his slightly dubious son.

Launching the car with a razzle-dazzle show, Tucker was his own high-powered emcee.

Tucker-owners both, Coppola and Lucas stood for a publicity picture before Coppola's gleaming burgundy-colored model (opposite). The majority of the 50 Tuckers that were made are still in operating condition.

THE LAND BEFORE TIME (1988)

Lucas's interest in all forms of animation, reflected in his support of John Korty's *Twice Upon a Time,* made him quickly receptive when Steven Spielberg proposed that he become involved in *The Land Before Time,* a project Spielberg was developing with Don Bluth.

A few years earlier, Bluth had left Disney and taken several of his fellow animators with him. Like Bluth, they were all restless and impatient with what they had come to feel were the limitations on their work at Disney. Bluth's approach to animation is more traditional than Korty's, but it involves taking traditional so-called full animation to higher technical levels than before. The Bluth team's first feature was *The Secret of NIMH,* based on a prize-winning children's book and dazzling in its shimmering, glittering effects of water, shadow, and light—the hardest things to create in animation. Their first collaboration with Spielberg had been the delightful adventures of an emigré family of mice, *An American Tail.*

"Steve had an idea about baby dinosaurs," Lucas says, "and he wanted me to executive produce it with him." Lucas sat in on the original story conferences with Spielberg, Kathleen Kennedy, and Frank Marshall, who were producing the film, and the writer, Stu Krieger. Judy Freudberg and Tony Geiss had done the basic story.

In *The Land Before Time,* the climate is changing and the green lands where the dinosaurs have been living are drying up. They must migrate to a new land, a fertile valley somewhere beyond the mountains. A charming baby brontosaurus called Littlefoot and his mother set out to make the perilous journey, which is beset with primeval creatures, notably the tyrannosaurus rex, who is unfriendly to dinosaurs of any size. Littlefoot's mother is killed in a series of giant earthquakes, and Littlefoot, now orphaned, has to carry on alone.

It is clear that Bluth and company did not leave the Disney influence entirely behind them. The baby dinosaurs are as winsomely anthropomorphic as any creatures in Disney. But the parched and tormented landscapes, in their ominous reds, browns, and grays, are something else again, far more sustained in their brooding severity than the somewhat comparable storms in *Fantasia. The Land Before Time* is a curious mixture of light charm and dark intensity, fairy-tale humor and a sobering sermon on the ruthless powers of nature.

"Animation is a completely different process from live action," Kathleen Kennedy says. "You formulate the script as you go through a certain amount of production. As the project begins to come to life, you have more ideas. It unlocks the door to imagination because you can do anything."

Kennedy admits they worried that the story was thin. Yet its basic messages were strong. "One woman wrote us that she'd had a hard time trying to explain to her little girl about the death of her father. She found that *Land Before Time* allowed her to explain, in much the same way that I suppose *Bambi* can help."

There were other themes that Kennedy feels gave the film strength. "The empowerment of children is a real central theme. Littlefoot is empowered. That's the theme, basically, in *ET* as well. And the theme of abandonment runs through a lot of fairy tales. Bettelheim said the fear of abandonment is the universal primal fear of most children. When those themes are explored in movies, they conjure up real feelings, even in adults, though you may not understand why."

THE LAND BEFORE TIME

Don Bluth (in foreground at top) and two of his animators go over the storyboards for the film.

Bluth, who with other animators broke away from Disney, grins amid the dinosaurs large and small he created.

INDIANA JONES AND THE LAST CRUSADE (1989)

George Lucas, Steven Spielberg says, "is smarter than I am about a lot of stuff. George is a better storyteller than I am. He loves to collaborate, and he collaborated all the way with me on the Indy pictures. He was very much involved in the editing on all three. If I'm getting into a project with or without George, I'll ask him to read the script, and I'll say, 'George, what do you think about this? What am I getting myself into?' He's my most generous friend."

"Steven and I have very similar tastes," Lucas agrees, "so it's very easy for us to work together. If we disagree about something, we both instantly defer to the other, but 90 percent of the time we agree on everything. And half the time we don't even have to talk about decisions."

The toughest aspect of the Indiana Jones trilogy was keeping costs in line. *Raiders of the Lost Ark* in 1980 cost $18 million. *Indiana Jones and the Temple of Doom,* shot three years later, cost $30 million. "Same crew, same number of shooting days, everything the same," Lucas says "That's the inflation between those two pictures."

Five years later, the budget Lucas presented to Paramount for *Indiana Jones and the Last Crusade* was for $44 million, and at first the studio balked. Lucas pointed out that the crew and shooting schedule would be the same as before and that the talent, or "above-the-line," cost (notably Spielberg, Lucas, Harrison Ford, and Sean Connery) would be less than 20 percent of the cost. "That's quite extraordinary," Lucas remarks. "And I said, 'I can tell you how many widgets we'll need, and what they'll cost.'" The budget was approved, and the film was delivered, as Lucas said it would be, for $44 million.

What to do for the third story had been a problem. Lucas had first envisioned what he called "a haunted-house movie." "But Steven had done *Poltergeist,* and he didn't want to do another movie like that." Lucas proposed a story based on a quest for the Holy Grail, but Spielberg felt the object of the quest was not tangible enough. Lucas then proposed a different story, adapted from a Chinese legend but involving the Monkey King in Africa. That sounded so promising that Lucas and two of Spielberg's producing associates, Frank Marshall and Kathleen Kennedy, went to Africa and scouted locations.

Chris Columbus wrote a script, but neither Lucas nor Spielberg was comfortable with the story. Lucas then had a new idea, reverting to the Holy Grail concept, and he wrote a memo about it. An initial draft of a script by Menno Meyjes still failed to convince

THE LAST CRUSADE

Galloping to the rescue of his father (opposite), Harrison Ford, wearing Indy's trademark slouch hat, blazes away on horseback.

Family ties link Sean Connery as Indy's father and Ford, trapped in a burning castle in one of the film's countless crises.

Spielberg. Then, when Meyjes went off to do another film, Jeff Boam was brought in to write a final version, and, Lucas says, "we licked it with Boam."

Lucas had introduced the idea of Indy's father as a character. It was Spielberg's inspiration to hire Sean Connery as the father. Lucas confesses that it was done "over my reservations. I thought his presence would unbalance the movie."

For his part, Spielberg had reservations about starting the film with a flashback to Indy as a boy. "Steven had been really trashed by the critics for *Empire of the Sun,* and he said, 'I just don't want to do any more films with kids in them.' I said, 'It's only ten minutes. No big deal.'" Boam's final script overcame Spielberg's hesitations.

The movie is a double homage: to the books, like Robert Louis Stevenson's *Kidnapped,* that generations of young people have loved and, once again, to the great adventure movies and serials.

Spielberg's casting of Connery, and the chiding, competitive, but loving relationship between father and son that Lucas and Boam had created (in very economical moments of dialogue) became a large plus for the movie and spared it from the charge that it was only a succession of thrills. At that, the thrills were once again sensational, not least some airplane and dirigible sequences, and an exploration in the rat-infested catacombs (imaginary) beneath Venice.

"There's a certain discipline that is established when you get into sequels," Lucas says. "It's like a sonnet or a haiku. There are things you're obliged to do or you're not doing what people want. I don't like working in an established form. I prefer to roam around, creatively. But once you develop a certain style and genre, you have to be faithful to it. I think I took both those genres, the *Star Wars* and the Indiana Jones pieces, much further than one would expect. But to go beyond that is very difficult."

Steven, says Lucas, "is a good friend, and we think so much alike that there were rumors that we were the same person. At a science-fiction convention somebody said that we were never seen in the same place at the same time. There was a rumor that we were one alien being, who could change form."

People occasionally congratulate Spielberg for *Star Wars* and credit Lucas with *ET.* "I don't bother to correct people anymore," Spielberg says, "and I occasionally sign George's name when I'm asked for an autograph."

THE LAST CRUSADE

Escorting yet another leading lady, Alison Doody as Elsa Schneider (opposite), Indy leads her into a ratty and skeleton-filled catacomb beneath Venice.

Hitching a lift on a German tank (top), Indy clings to a gun barrel and seems to contemplate getting into another line of work.

Elsa fights off the spidery fingers of a villain who has sipped the wrong drink and lost his composure completely.

THE LAST CRUSADE

As the young Indy in Boy Scout uniform, River Phoenix (top) escapes a truckful of tomb looters who are after the Cross of Coronado.

Bullwhip, another trademark, at his belt, Indy scrambles up a tank, aiming to rescue his captured father and, as usual, hold his own against overpowering odds.

Making a splash in Venice, Indy prepares to escape in a powerboat before he is chewed up by giant propellers.

**Keeping up with the Joneses, the Nazi villains pursue
Indy and his father in a fighter plane.**

THE LAST CRUSADE

Loving but quarrelsome (top), the father-son relationship gave the film an additional charm.

Zapping a zeppelin crewman, Indy starts a fight when, as a stowaway, he can't produce a ticket in midair.

"MANIAC MANSION" [1990]

Unquestionably, the wildest offshoot of a Lucas enterprise has been the highly successful television series "Maniac Mansion," which began life as a very popular computer game devised in the Lucasfilm Games Division.

The really weird family of Edisons (an ironic nod to Thomas Alva if ever there was one) and their mansion full of gadgetries, infernal and otherwise, came to television from the satiric imaginations of the SCTV comedy troupe. It made its debut on the Family Channel in September 1990, and *Time* magazine hailed it as one of the year's best television offerings.

Its pleasures continue to include four-year-old Turner Edison, who is the size of a professional wrestler; the teenagers Ike and Tina Edison; Aunt Idella, who is relatively normal in stature; and Uncle Harry, who has translucent wings and is about the size of a healthy gerbil. Dr. Fred Edison and his wife, Casey, are about as ordinary as parents can be with a meteorite in their basement.

Peter Sussman, Eugene Levy, and Barry Jossen are the executive producers of "Maniac Mansion," with Seaton McLean and Michael Short as supervising producers and Jamie Paul Rock as producer.

The series is a coproduction of Atlantis Films, the Family Channel itself, YTV/Canada, Inc., and Lucasfilm Ltd. Television.

"MANIAC MANSION"

The bizarre Edison family (below), with Joe Flaherty as Dr. Fred, looks aghast at the latest disaster wrought by the meteorite in the basement.

Flaherty and Martin Short (opposite), who makes a guest appearance on the show, both came out of the SCTV comedy troupe.

THE ADVENTURES OF INDIANA JONES AS A YOUNG MAN

"The Young Indiana Jones Chronicles," a television series that made its first appearance in 1992, was, as Lucas said at the time, "only the tip of the iceberg." The series had grown out of his passionate belief in the educational potential of interactive multimedia television—television linked with a computer in which the viewer is a participant rather than a passive watcher.

Lucas previously had founded the George Lucas Educational Foundation to explore and develop the possibilities of the videodisc combining text, sound, and both still and moving graphics, all at the user's command via the computer keyboard or mouse.

"We were working on an idea called 'A Walk through Early-Twentieth-Century History with Indiana Jones,' and it turned into a television series," Lucas said.

"It's a series of ideas, as well as action. I think people need to be exposed to all kinds of information, hopefully in entertaining form, so they have an opportunity to understand the larger world of ideas."

Lucas was the executive producer of the project and generated all the basic stories. But the television format really was only the beginning of a bold three-stage evolution. The television material (some of it never actually seen on television) has been reedited and expanded into the twenty-two stunning feature-length movies described on these pages. These films will be available on videotape as *The Adventures of Indiana Jones As a Young Man.*

Then, finally, as the so-called DVD-format high-density discs with their great storage capacity become widely available, the movies will be further expanded into truly interactive, multimedia experiences— entertaining and painlessly educational.

The stories follow Indy (born in 1899) from age nine to his midtwenties and engage him with the major events and personalities of the early twentieth century. "Each of the stories has a subject," Lucas says, "and in a very few years, when you get the multimedia version, the one on jazz, let's say, will offer files on Louis Armstrong and Sidney Bechet, Al Capone and Prohibition and speakeasies. And there'll be mystery-adventure multimedia choices that will allow viewers to go off on their own, learning—in the case of that particular episode—to read music, even to play jazz.

"It's all ten years ahead of its time, but I realized I had a chance to do part of it now, the biggest part of it. We'll add the rest when the new digital format is available. I don't consider anything ever really finished."

Doing *Young Indy* was an extraordinary undertaking. Rick McCallum, the producer on the project, says, "We ended up shooting over 170 weeks—more than three years—on locations in

George Lucas on the set of a New York episode.

twenty-five countries. It's the longest sustained period of shooting in the history of either film or television. We have 4 million feet of 16mm film; that's more than 750 miles worth, from New Guinea to Thailand to Greece, Russia, all of Europe, Turkey, North Africa, and Kenya." The last of the shooting was completed in Morocco as recently as mid-1996.

The crews endured fierce heat in Spain and subzero cold in the Czech Republic, narrowly escaped harm from an avalanche in the Italian Alps, were filming near the epicenter when the Northridge earthquake hit, received death threats in Turkey, miraculously escaped injuries or worse when a boat capsized in a crocodile-filled African river. They rode donkeys to remote locations and lived in tent encampments for weeks on end. For all of them, it was a welcome exposure to a new approach to filmmaking.

Indeed, beyond the long-range intentions for the product itself, Lucas seized on the making of *Young Indy* as a time for experimenting with many new production techniques, in particular what he calls "nonlinear filmmaking." Instead of the traditional three-stage process—preproduction, production, postproduction—in nonlinear production all three stages go on, to some extent, concurrently.

"You get to work on drafts of shooting and editing," Lucas says, "just as the industry has always done drafts of screenplays. Since we always had a standing crew, we could reshoot stuff while we were editing. We could go back and add things and make things clearer." Some of the films took more than three years to complete from first shot to last.

The nonlinear approach to production and the wide geographic range of locations—often within the same film—made the creation of *The Adventures of Indiana Jones As a Young Man* even more collaborative than filmmaking always is. So it is that many of the films are credited to more than one director and more than one writer. Given the freedom to treat each episode as one reel in a larger film, the crews could shoot scenes as needed, sending the film back to Lucas in California to edit and suggest changes and additions. These new parts could be shot weeks or months later, perhaps in another country. The whole experience was "unprecedented and liberating," according to producer McCallum.

The adventures of Young Indy sweep across the world and the twentieth century, with a cavalcade of historical figures from Leo Tolstoy and Sigmund Freud to Mata Hari and George Gershwin. The scripts are the work of a corps of well-known and honored writers for film and television, many of whom met at Skywalker Ranch for long plotting sessions with Lucas. ("They were very lively," Lucas says fondly.) The directors, too, were an honor roll of the industry's best. Joining young Corey Carrier as the child Indy and Sean Patrick Flanery as the older Indy was a supporting cast of international stars, including Vanessa Redgrave, Max von Sydow, Pernilla August, Dorothy Tutin, Terry Jones, Peter Firth, Joss Ackland, Lukas Haas, Elizabeth Hurley, John Wood, Jeroen Krabbe, Anna Massey, Timothy Spall, and John Lynch. The series employed a virtual United Nations of crewmen—some twenty nationalities, from Kenyans to Thais.

Shooting the *Young Indy* series was not least an enormously significant opportunity to employ the fast-evolving technology of digital effects to reduce costs and at the same time to increase the size and the apparent resources of the production.

"We were creating the world at the beginning of the twentieth century," Rick McCallum says, "and some of the effects didn't even play as effects. They involved painting out buildings and telephone wires, coping with all the problems you usually have working on locations."

But the technology also produced miracles of multiplication. "We were shooting in Spain and we only had four riders," says McCallum. "We needed to make them look like thirty-five or forty riders, and thanks to digital we did." In another of the films, Indy is stage manager of a Gershwin musical. "We had six dancers; made 'em look like 125. We had one vintage car. It became eight or nine."

In the end, says George Lucas, "What we have are twenty-two feature films, done on a TV schedule, and that's what we set out to do. The films are very handsome, with big action sequences, and they're all period. And the cost of each was under 4 million dollars. So we have twenty-two features done at a cost of one big movie feature today. They're now titled as movies; they'll play as movies."

And for the longer run, the lessons learned in nonlinear filmmaking and the further uses of digital technology will affect the making of the next *Star Wars* trilogy and indeed all the further Lucas ventures.

Lucas's daughter, Katie, working with her father on a *Young Indy* location in Spain.

My First Adventure

Directors: Jim O'Brien, Michael Schultz
Writers: Jonathan Hales, Jule Selbo

In the earliest glimpse of the really young Young Indy, he is nine (above)—it is 1908—and along on his father's lecture tour around the world. At an archaeological dig in the Valley of the Kings in Egypt, Indy finds an ancient mummy and a fresh corpse, and with help from Lawrence of Arabia he solves a mystery. For his pains, he is kidnapped by slave traders and hauled across the Sahara to the slave market at Marrakech, where he must use all his wits to escape. Lawrence communicates the excitements of archaeology—a lesson Indy obviously will not forget. The nonlinear shooting meant that Corey Carrier was actually fifteen by the time the film's last sequences in Africa were shot, but some digital wizardry in postproduction erased the changes in his looks. The film won Emmys in 1992 for art direction, costume design, editing, and makeup.

Passion for Life

Directors: Carl Schultz, Rene Manzor
Writers: Matthew Jacobs, Reg Gadney

Teddy Roosevelt, Norman Rockwell, Edgar Degas, and Pablo Picasso all enter Young Indy's life and contribute to an education he'd never have received in fourth grade. He first goes on safari to the Masai Mara game preserve in Kenya with "T.R." and becomes lost in the vast and dangerous wilderness. Later, in Paris, he runs into the young Norman Rockwell (played by Lukas Haas, who starred in *Witness*). Together they explore the fine-art scene and the rather wilder café scenes of Montmartre (upper right), where they watch and listen as Degas and Picasso argue violently about what

painting is. After using Prague for some scenes, the production moved to Paris with fifty extras (for visual continuity) and, with a small, six-person crew, shot documentary-like footage around the Louvre and other locations for authenticity (and to keep costs down).

The Perils of Cupid

Directors: Bille August, Mike Newell
Writers: Matthew Jacobs, Jule Selbo

Love—well, first infatuation—smites Young Indy in colorful Old Vienna (above), where he falls for the daughter of Archduke Francis Ferdinand, who later will be assassinated (the event that precipitated the onset of World War I). Needing emotional guidance in his own crisis, Indy sounds out Sigmund Freud (played by Max von Sydow) and Carl Jung on what love is all about. In Florence, love problems show up in another way as Indy's mother is smitten with Giacomo Puccini, composer of such Romantic operas as *La Bohème* and *Tosca*, and Indy himself must scheme to be an "unmatchmaker" and get Mama safely home to Daddy. The film was shot in several glorious locations, not only Florence, but also Pisa, Prague, the Dolomite Mountains in Italy, and in Stockholm (where Max von Sydow was living). Bille August directed *Pelle the Conqueror*; Mike Newell did *Four Weddings and a Funeral*.

Travels with Father

Directors: Michael Schultz, Deepa Mehta
Writers: Frank Darabont, Matthew Jacobs, Jonathan Hales

Young Indy's amazing geographic odyssey (the viewer's, too) continues as the lad, now a headstrong eleven, runs away from his parents in Russia. He meets the famous novelist Leo Tolstoy and they travel together, talking philosophy and warding off Gypsies and fierce Cossacks. Shaken and eager for the security of family, Indy rejoins his parents and they head for Athens. He and his father visit a monastery deliberately situated on a forbidding mountaintop. They make the white-knuckle trip up the thousand-foot face of the mountain in a tiny cage, an experience that leads to a heavy father-son bonding. Once again, the story offers food for thought as well as a feast for the eyes. The crew, feeling like gypsy filmmakers, worked in Russia, Poland, the Czech Republic, and Greece; in Greece alone they shot in fourteen different locations, including the Acropolis (above). The actual cage was photographed in Meteori, and the action was created digitally in Prague and London.

Journey of Radiance

Directors: Deepa Mehta, Gavin Millar
Writers: Jonathan Hensleigh, Rosemary Anne Sisson

The elder Jones's lecture tour takes Young Indy and his parents to India, where Indy learns about having faith in oneself from the Theosophist philosopher Jiddu Krishnamurti. Later on in China, where Indy falls desperately ill with typhoid fever, his mother learns more lessons in faith and trust from villagers whose ancient medicines must save the boy's life—if they can. Shot in Banaras, India, and China, the film was codirected by the Indian-born Deepa Mehta

(*Sam and Me*) and Gavin Millar (*DreamChild*), a Scot. As in all the Young Indy films, the sights and sounds of real locations—teeming India, rural China—give the story unforgettable authenticity. And, once again, Indy's adventures are mind-broadening as well as physical. According to producer Rick McCallum, it offered the most moving experiences of the production's first year: the sight of the Ganges and its thousands of worshipers at dawn, and traveling on donkeys to film the Great Wall of China (above) in locations few foreigners had visited in fifty years.

Spring Break Adventure

Directors: Joe Johnston, Carl Schultz
Writers: Matthew Jacobs, Jonathan Hales

Historical figures careen through this swift and eventful story. The year is 1916 and Indy has a girlfriend—Nancy Stratemeyer, whose father, Edward L. Stratemeyer, was the creator of Nancy Drew. The couple visit Thomas Edison and are quickly entangled with German spies who are hot after one of Edison's inventions that has great strategic value. Later, visiting an aunt in New Mexico during spring break, Indy is kidnapped by Pancho Villa and swept up in the Mexican Revolution (above). There's a train robbery in true Wild West style and a barroom encounter with a dashing young cavalry officer named

George Patton. With all its excitement, the film is also a fascinating introduction to the Mexican Revolution and its vivid central figure, Villa. Much of the film was shot in 130-degree weather in Spain, on locations used by *Lawrence of Arabia*. It was the series' first major use of digital effects; more than one hundred effects were employed, including multiplying four horsemen into three dozen. There were Emmys in 1992 for art direction, costume design, editing, and makeup. Codirector Joe Johnston is a former ILM designer who directed *Honey, I Shrunk the Kids* and *Jumanji*. Jacobs adapted *Lassie* in 1994.

Love's Sweet Song
Directors: Gillies MacKinnon, Carl Schultz
Writers: Jonathan Hales, Rosemary Anne Sisson

Ireland's bloody Easter Rebellion in 1916, the suffragette movement in England, a Zeppelin raid (one of history's first air bombardments), and a meeting with a rising young British cabinet officer named Winston Churchill become vivid episodes in Indy's life (above). So do Indy's brief but impassioned romances, first with a colleen whose brother proves to be one of the clandestine Irish rebels and then with an Englishwoman who decides that the vote comes before love. The movie was shot in London, with costars Elizabeth Hurley and the Academy Award–winning actress Vanessa Redgrave. Later digital magic turned fifteen extras into crowds of hundreds. MacKinnon directed *The Playboys*. Rosemary Anne Sisson wrote *Upstairs, Downstairs*.

The Trenches of Hell
Director: Simon Wincer
Writer: Jonathan Hensleigh

Despite the modest budgets on which the Indy films were made, the Lucas team re-created the horrors of the trench warfare of

World War I with astonishing realism and on a large scale (above). In August 1916, Indy is a soldier in the Belgian Army at the Battle of the Somme, one of the war's bloodiest, with more than a million casualties on both sides. Indy endures artillery barrages and nerve-gas attacks, then is captured by the Germans. In the prison camp he plans his escape with a young French officer named Charles de Gaulle. The dramatic film won an Emmy in 1993 for sound editing. Writer Jonathan Hensleigh also wrote *Die Hard with a Vengeance*.

Demons of Deception
Directors: Rene Manzor, Nicolas Roeg
Writers: Jonathan Hensleigh, Carrie Fisher

A dramatic shift from the go-for-broke thrills of some of Indy's other adventures, this film, set in 1916, looks hard at the horrors of war and at the callous stupidity of German officers who sent thousands of men to their deaths at Verdun and Passchendaele for virtually no territorial gain. Indy must ponder the moral dilemmas of leadership, even as he falls deeply in love with the German spy Mata Hari, only to suffer the pains of disillusionment and deceit. Shot largely in Prague in temperatures that fell below zero, the film (above) is both action-filled and mature and thoughtful. It was codirected by Nicolas Roeg (*Walkabout, Don't Look Now*) and one of the authors was actress and novelist Carrie Fisher. The film won an Emmy in 1992 for sound mixing.

Phantom Train of Doom

Director: Peter MacDonald
Writer: Frank Darabont

Shot entirely on location in Kenya and set in German East Africa in November 1916, amid the brutal struggles of World War I, this thrilling tale sends Indy (Sean Patrick Flanery) to Africa, where he is to meet a small, daring band of sixty-five-plus-year-old soldiers who call themselves "The Old and the Bold." Crossing enemy-held land by wagon train and, in a dazzling cinematic sequence, by hot-air balloon, their mission is to destroy a massive German artillery piece. Tracing the gun to the mountain cave where it is concealed, they risk their lives, as in *The Guns of Navarone*, to destroy it. To create a period train, the crew built sets on top of modern rolling stock, and, in general, the visual effects were spectacular (above). Cast and crew lived in a tent compound in Kenya for weeks; they even grew their own vegetables. The film won an Emmy nomination for sound mixing in 1992. Director Peter MacDonald did *Rambo III* and writer Frank Darabont wrote and directed *The Shawshank Redemption*.

Oganga: The Giver and Taker of Life

Director: Simon Wincer
Writer: Frank Darabont

It is 1916–17 and Indy is on a vital mission through Africa for the Allies. In a village ravaged by an epidemic, Indy rescues a child from certain death. But as he fights his way cross-country, Indy's mission is endangered by the child, and he faces a moral quandary and a test of conscience. He then encounters the legendary doctor-musician-philosopher Albert Schweitzer and, working with Schweitzer at his hospital, he rediscovers his own humanity and reaffirms his personal values. This unusually beautiful and thoughtful film was shot in the Congo (upper right). In the most dramatic of the incidents to occur

during filming, a boat sailing in a river near the Somalia border struck a sandbar and capsized, throwing the whole cast, including one hundred extras, into crocodile-infested waters. The crocodiles were evidently startled away, and there was not a single injury.

Attack of the Hawkmen

Director: Ben Burtt
Writers: Matthew Jacobs, Rosemary Anne Sisson, Ben Burtt

World War I was the first time the airplane was used as a military weapon, and in 1917 Young Indy is quickly and predictably airborne in the Allied cause (above). He learns to fly and, working with the French Secret Service, joins the famous Lafayette Escadrille, in which many Americans served. Scouting behind German lines, he is shot down by Manfred von Richthofen—the Red Baron of both historical and Snoopy fame. Their aerial battle is a dazzling sequence in the great tradition of *Wings*. On foot in enemy territory Indy encounters the German aircraft designer Anthony Fokker and learns about a secret weapon that could lead to German victory, unless... Locations in the Czech Republic, France, and Germany give the film a strong feeling of authenticity. In another demonstration of digital magic, the aerial dogfights were all created in the computer with models. Ben Burtt did the sound effects for *Star Wars*, *E.T.*, and other films before turning to directing.

Adventures in the Secret Service
Directors: Vic Armstrong, Simon Wincer
Writers: Frank Darabont, Gavin Scott

With ILM's visual effects wizardry complementing actual location shoots in Vienna and St. Petersburg, this film captures Indy's daring deeds as a spy sent by the Allies on a dangerous mission behind enemy lines to the palace of Habsburg emperor Charles I, ruler of war-weary Austria. Indy moves on to an even more perilous assignment in revolutionary Russia, where he infiltrates a Bolshevik organization, endangering himself and his friends, and is forced to make hard choices between duty and friendship. The film (above and below) is a forceful visual introduction to the chaos in the last stages of World War I as a new Soviet Union and a changed map of Europe were emerging; ironically, the Soviet Union itself was disintegrating as the film was being made. Disconcertingly, Russian soldiers offered to sell the crew a Scud missile for $10,000, and a nuclear power plant blew up near a filming location. Coauthor Gavin Scott's earlier credits include *The Mummy* for Paramount.

Espionage Escapades
Directors: Terry Jones, Robert Young
Writer: Gavin Scott

A delicious change of pace from Indy's more serious entanglements, this film—codirected by and starring Terry Jones of the Monty Python troupe—takes wonderfully potty potshots at the suave posturing of most espionage films and at the numbing stupidity of bureaucrats everywhere (above and below). Posing as a dancer for the Ballets Russes in Barcelona in 1917, Indy meets his old friend Pablo Picasso, narrowly outwits some inept German spies, and whisks off to Prague, where his assignment is to get a telephone and wait for a call—a bureaucratic impossibility until Franz Kafka volunteers to help. The rich variety of the Young Indy films was never better demonstrated and, as always, the film was shot on location, this time in Spain and Prague.

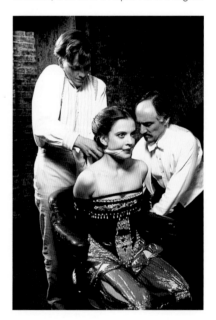

Tales of Innocence

Directors: Bille August, Michael Schultz
Writer: Jonathan Hales

Set in 1917 and photographed in both Italy and Morocco, *Tales of Innocence* (above) finds Indy's life complicated by his incurable romanticism, as he competes with a young American journalist named Ernest Hemingway for the love of a gorgeous Italian girl. Now a spy for the Allies, Indy goes behind enemy lines hoping to bring off a propaganda coup that might shorten the war. Wounded in action, he makes his way to North Africa, where he is assigned to join the French Foreign Legion to root out a traitor. There is action aplenty as Indy battles Berber tribesmen. Ever the romantic, he has a brief encounter with the novelist Edith Wharton. Shooting in the Dolomite Mountains in northern Italy, the company barely missed being buried beneath a late-season avalanche. Codirector Bille August's other credits include *Pelle the Conqueror* and *The House of the Spirits*. Jonathan Hales adapted Agatha Christie's *The Mirror Crack'd*.

Daredevils of the Desert

Director: Simon Wincer
Writer: Frank Darabont

The amazing scale of the Young Indiana Jones adventures is exemplified by this tumultuous tale of desert warfare in the Middle East during World War I, which culminates in a screen-filling cavalry charge by the Australian Lighthorsemen Regiment. The year is 1917 and Indy is sent to assist the Australians as they attack the ancient town of Beersheba (upper right). He enlists the help of a belly dancer in a suspenseful mission to defuse the explosives with which the occupying Turks have booby-trapped the city's water supply. The film was nearly three years in production, with shooting not only in Turkey, but also in Prague, Kenya, North Carolina, and

Arizona, whenever the cast principals could be reassembled for additional scenes. It was at times a dangerous experience, with death threats from the Islamic Jihad in Turkey and war tensions on the Iraqi border. Simon Wincer directed television's *Lonesome Dove*.

Masks of Evil

Directors: Mike Newell, Dick Maas
Writers: Rosemary Anne Sisson, Jonathan Hensleigh

The film could be subtitled *Young Indy vs. The Vampires*. Passing through Transylvania in 1918, Indy encounters the original vampire, Vlad the Impaler, centuries old but kept young and vigorous by his do-it-yourself transfusions. Vlad and his legions of the undead bent on world domination give Indy the toughest, weirdest battle of his life. Earlier, on assignment for French Intelligence in an Istanbul thick with spies and danger, Indy fights a Turkish plot to assassinate French agents (above). The Istanbul locations and the brooding Transylvania mountains where vampires seem entirely believable give *Masks of Evil* a fine and scary power. Shot in Poland and the Czech Republic as well as Istanbul, the film has an unusual glimpse of the legendary Whirling Dervishes performing. Principal director Mike Newell did both *Enchanted April* and *Four Weddings and a Funeral*. Dutch codirector Dick Maas did *Rigor Mortis* and *Amsterdamned*.

Treasure of the Peacock's Eye
Director: Carl Schultz
Writer: Jule Selbo

In a globe-spanning, swashbuckling, fast-action, surprise-crammed thriller (above and below) in the tradition of the Indiana Jones feature films, Young Indy takes off in search of a legendary diamond said to have belonged to Alexander the Great. The quest begins when a dying man gasps, "The eye of the Peacock!" Indy is stalked by a ruthless, one-eyed man as he races from London to Egypt to the South Seas, where he becomes embroiled in a vicious shipboard battle with Chinese pirates (talk about swashbuckling!). Marooned on a remote island, Indy is captured by cannibalistic natives, and only the timely arrival of the famous anthropologist Bronislaw Malinowski gives him a fighting chance to save his skin—and his head. The production moved to the Trobriand Islands off southeast New Guinea and then took native extras back to Thailand, where the boat was re-created for further scenes. Director Carl Schultz did *Careful, He Might Hear You;* writer Jule Selbo's many credits include *Tales from the Darkside*.

Winds of Change
Directors: David Hare, Michael Schultz
Writer: Jonathan Hales

It is 1919. World War I is over, and Indy, by now fluent in several languages, is working as a translator at the Paris Peace Conference, giving him—and the viewer—a ringside seat at a history-making and controversial event (above). The figures in view include Lawrence of Arabia, Prince Faisal of Arabia, and Ho Chi Minh, who was to loom large in American lives a few decades later. Back in Princeton, New Jersey, disillusioned by the hard and cynical realities of international politics, Indy discovers home-style bigotry cruelly touching his boyhood friend Paul Robeson. Major digital effects made twenty extras become fifteen hundred in the astonishing Versailles conference scenes. Like all the Young Indy films, *Winds of Change* brings history alive in a way that is both dramatic and accurate. British director David Hare's credits include *Wetherby*.

Mystery of the Blues
Director: Carl Schultz
Writer: Jule Selbo

Chicago at its most toddlin'—Prohibition, speakeasies, gangsters (Al Capone principally among them), and above all the joys of jazz—makes Indy's return to peacetime life and a belated crack at college as lively, and dangerous, as it ever was. He's working at a down-and-dirty speak where the great Sidney Bechet teaches him to play jazz. Indy's college roommate Eliot Ness, not yet an Untouchable, helps him solve a nasty murder that gets him out of an ominous beef with Capone. American society, vintage 1920, comes alive with its special blend of vigor and violence, all to the syncopated beat of the new art form called jazz. After all the foreign

adventures, *Mystery of the Blues* (above) was made largely at studios in North Carolina and cast with local people. The film won 1993 Emmys for cinematography, music direction, and sound mixing.

Scandal of 1920

Director: Syd Macartney
Writer: Jonathan Hales

There's obviously no limit to Indy's versatility, nor to the range of situations in which he finds himself. Here, in a wonderful tribute to the American musical, Indy, on a summer break from college, is stage-managing a new work by George Gershwin (above). The film's dazzling visual effects include a Broadway theater that never was (inside or out), street scenes to be found on no known map, and 6 dancers transformed into choruses of 30, 60, and finally 120, for loopy and lavish production numbers in the spirit of 1920s Broadway. Indy even gets to trade quips with the famed and razor-witted Algonquin Round Table when he is not soothing temperamental stars, romancing three different women at once, and worrying about suspicious backstage malfunctionings. It's a smashing piece of social and cultural history. The film won 1993 Emmys for costume design, music composition, and special visual effects. The Irish director Syd Macartney previously directed *The Bridge*.

Hollywood Follies

Director: Michael Schultz
Writers: Jonathan Hales, Matthew Jacobs

It was inevitable that Indy would find his way to Tinsel Town, and in this film the viewer has the feeling that everybody involved had a fine time tossing darts at the studios and their bizarre ways. Trying to earn money for his college tuition, Indy has a summer job as a junior executive at a studio and fights a losing battle with the imperious Erich von Stroheim over the skyrocketing costs of *Foolish Wives* (1922). Stifled by the system, Indy goes on location with John Ford, and even gets to shine before the cameras (below). The team, shooting in nearby Fillmore when the devastating Northridge earthquake hit in 1994, worked footage of a major aftershock into the story. The gently satiric film won 1995 Emmy nominations for special visual effects and for music composition. Michael Schultz's many films include *Car Wash* and *Sgt. Pepper's Lonely Hearts Club Band*.

RADIOLAND MURDERS (1994)

The idea that became *Radioland Murders* first took shape in the early 1970s while Lucas was simultaneously filming *American Graffiti* and beginning to write the first *Star Wars* trilogy.

"I wanted to do an out-and-out comedy; I thought of *Graffiti* as an amusing slice of life rather than a comedy," says Lucas. "And I wanted to do something off-the-wall and crazy, in the tradition of Abbott and Costello. Since I was working on a movie about radio at the time, I decided to do the comedy about radio. So *Radioland Murders* became a project."

Years later, working on the *Young Indy* films and experimenting with his new production techniques, Lucas wondered whether what worked for the smaller television screen, and was easy and inexpensive, could translate to the movie screen, with its demand for higher resolution. He decided the way to find out was indeed to make a movie, and *Radioland Murders* was ready and waiting.

A farce about a radio station with a whiz-bang variety show, where evil is afoot and murder rears its improbable head, *Radioland Murders* catches the knockabout pace of the comedies of the 1930s with pursuits, chases, and rising hysteria. Mel Smith was the director.

"We shot it for the wide theater screen, as of course the new *Star Wars* films will be, to test our new techniques further," Lucas says. The story involved a lot of sets, as *Young Indy*, which was shot entirely on location, did not. "We wanted to build sets that were partly for real and partly digital, to see how they all fit together." Amazingly, the film's major action sequence, involving characters hanging from the exterior of an office building and ending on a radio tower commanding a sweeping view of the city below, was done entirely on a sound stage in North Carolina. It is, in the newest, truest sense, movie magic.

Yet the film did poorly at the box office. "Here was a low-concept movie with no movie stars in it," Lucas says, "and the response to it was disappointing to say the least. I'm still amazed that *Star Wars* did as well as it did, and I'm just as amazed that *Radioland Murders* did as poorly as it did. Somehow you expect them to land in the middle somewhere. But if you can't get a trademark name in there and a concept that's mostly high-action adventure, it's very hard to get anyone to go to the theater anymore. I still enjoy *Radioland* a lot. It's lively, it's funny, and it's about a subject I like."

And as an experiment in production, it was a success. Given its production values and a cast that was not starry but loaded with fine and recognizable character actors doing cameos, its modest cost—about $10 million—was a remarkable demonstration of the cost-effectiveness of digital technology.

RADIOLAND MURDERS

Michael Lerner is a homicide detective and Brian Benben is an innocent in handcuffs trying to alert him to another murder in progress.

The imperious bemedaled boss of WBN, General Whalen (Ned Beatty), informs his staff that a couple of murders aren't going to stop his station from going on the air (opposite).

RADIOLAND MURDERS

Embattled protagonists Brian Benben and Mary Stuart Masterson (top) give the station's writers a pep talk.

Suspicious characters—producer, monocled station manager, and sound engineer (Robert Walden, Larry Miller, and Stephen Tobolowsky)—warily convene in the WBN control booth.

The big show for opening night (opposite) features a costumed accordion chorale led by beaming bandleader Rick Rochester (Michael McKean) in a gentle spoof of such events.

A DIRECTOR'S THREE WISHES:
THE STAR WARS TRILOGY SPECIAL EDITION

The extraordinary and persistent appeal of the *Star Wars* trilogy made it increasingly clear that there was a hunger among its followers to see the films again in their full glory—on theater screens. Then, too, there were millions of young people born since 1977 who had been able to see the films only on television screens.

Thus the decision was made to celebrate the twentieth anniversary of the premiere of *Star Wars* in 1977 by releasing all three films in rapid succession as the *Star Wars Trilogy Special Edition*. They would all be in theaters simultaneously, making it possible to enjoy George Lucas's epic virtually as the one continuous story it is.

There is a Hollywood tradition of rereleasing major films (*Gone With the Wind* has been released several times, once in a reedited wide-screen version). Often there are fresh prints and restored trims to produce what is called "the director's cut." But this practice all but stopped after the rise of the videocassette. Releasing all three of the *Star Wars* films on a large scale after they had been previously released on television and video was unprecedented—and a major undertaking.

Work on the project began in 1994, and the first and most frightening aspect of the project was the discovery that good negatives of the films were hard to find. The color in many negatives had deteriorated (a problem underscoring the urgency of the campaign for film preservation). "We had to call in prints from all over the world," says producer Rick McCallum, who worked closely with Lucas on the Special Edition. "We solved the problem, but it was a close call."

For Lucas personally, bringing out the films again was a wonderful opportunity to fulfill a long-standing dream. "I always wanted to fix the movies, which I think most directors want to do with their films," he says. "Go back and fix the things that were wrong because the directors had to meet deadlines."

From the beginning, Lucas had said that *Star Wars* was only 70 percent of the film he saw in his imagination—a remarkable statement in view of the film's enormous popularity and the impact it has had on the field of special effects.

STAR WARS TRILOGY SPECIAL EDITION

The stolen Imperial shuttle Tydirium speeds toward the forest moon of Endor in *Return of the Jedi*.

Lucas directs a far-out Rodian musician for the expanded version of the famous "Jedi Rocks" club scene in Jabba's palace in *Return of the Jedi* (opposite top). Dancing girls added to the scene are like none Vegas ever saw (left).

Melding old and new, ILM composited film of Ford from the original *Star Wars* with new computer images of a digital Jabba the Hutt now able to walk (opposite bottom).

Now, Lucas says, "I've been able to put all the things in there and fix all the things that I couldn't twenty years ago because I didn't have the technology, didn't have the money, didn't have the time." The three films now represent not the director's cut, Lucas says, "but the director's wish."

"We redid some of the music, recut some of the scenes, added new special effects and even whole scenes that were either not completed as I'd originally imagined them, or shot but not put into the movies because we didn't have the resources. We did most of the work on *Star Wars* [now bearing its original title, *Star Wars: A New Hope*] and *Return of the Jedi*."

On *The Empire Strikes Back,* the amazing snow battle on the ice planet Hoth has been re-composited with digital matting to make it look, as Lucas says, "the way people thought it looked in 1980."

For Lucas, perhaps the single most satisfying aspect of the revised version of *A New Hope* has been the time, technology, and money spent on making Jabba the Hutt fully mobile. "Before," says Lucas, "he was just a big rubber thing we had on this platform." Now, digitally created, Jabba has been inserted into existing footage to create entirely new scenes. "Now he actually walks across the floor of the docking bay with Harrison Ford, and it's great," Lucas says.

The walking Jabba is a teasing foretaste of the far greater mobility that familiar creations seem likely to have in Episodes One, Two, and Three, the prequel trilogy now in preparation. (*Star Wars: A New Hope, The Empire Strikes Back,* and *Return of the Jedi* were Episodes Four, Five, and Six.)

Looking ahead to the new episodes (but not giving too much away), Lucas says, "Now Yoda can walk; he couldn't in the earlier film. R2-D2 couldn't go anywhere; he could barely walk, and if he had to fix something with one of his little mechanical hands, it was very cumbersome. Neither R2-D2 nor C-3PO could go up and down stairs. It doesn't sound like much, but when you're writing a script, you're stuck. Now I'm much freer."

It is clear that the possibilities of digital technology that are presented to the filmmaker are mind-boggling·and even intimidating. But Lucas, as probably the truest auteur of the digital revolution, finds the possibilities wholly liberating.

"Science fiction is a very literary medium," Lucas says. "That's why it's so difficult to translate science-fiction novels into films, because film is a very literal medium. It's very hard to take fantasy ideas, ideas that don't exist, and put them into a real world and make them real. Yet somehow you do have to make them real for a moment. But now we can do it digitally, because the digital world is a much more literary world."

STAR WARS TRILOGY SPECIAL EDITION
Coruscant (below) celebrates the defeat of the Empire at the end of *Return of the Jedi*.

The Sarlacc hungrily awaits its prey in *Return of the Jedi* (opposite top).

Cloud City prepares for evacuation in *The Empire Strikes Back* (opposite bottom).

In *Star Wars: A New Hope*, the main drag in Mos Eisley is an extraordinary spectacle of droids, Jawas, humanoids, and even a swoop rider on a speeder bike in the path of a giant ronto (right).

Princess Leia paces before a window in Cloud City (above) in a new scene from *The Empire Strikes Back*.

A wild bantha herd (left) traverses the sandy Tatooine dunes in *Return of the Jedi*.

THE SKYWALKER RANCH

The original inspiration for what became Skywalker Ranch, Lucas says, sprang from his days at the University of Southern California film school in the 1960s. "At that time the school was a tiny enclave of creative people working together and having everything we needed to make movies in a pleasant environment. It was quite a bit different from the way the studios were set up, like large factories." Later his friend Francis Coppola visited several small, unfactory-like studios in Europe. "He'd seen one in Denmark that was in an old mansion. Francis said it was wonderful, like a boutique studio, without sound stages." That was what Lucas and Coppola both came to think would be ideal. "It would be," Lucas says, "like a big *home*, a big fraternity where filmmakers could work together and create together."

The whole concept, he adds, "was that you didn't need sound stages because you would shoot in the street. You need a place to create stories and you need a place to finish the movie, to do the postproduction sound and editing. It was the era of *Easy Rider* and moving vans with all the equipment in them. I wanted to free up filmmaking and have it more like a street adventure, guerrilla units instead of a crew of 150. Very 60s, very idealistic."

Their first combined effort, American Zoetrope, in a warehouse on Folsom Street in San Francisco, was office if not home to that "loose confederation of radicals and hippies," as Lucas described it years later. Lucas was living in a small rented house on a hilltop in Mill Valley. After Warner Brothers withdrew its financial support from Zoetrope, Lucas converted his attic into an editing room and one of the bedrooms into a sound-editing facility, and there worked on the postproduction of *THX 1138* and scripts for future films. Later he acquired a large Victorian house in San Anselmo, and it served as "home" for Lucas and other directors. It is now his home exclusively, his old office now the dining room.

Jane Bay, who had been administrative assistant to Jerry Brown in his candidate days, was hired by Lucas as executive assistant in the summer of 1977 and moved to Marin as one of only four Lucas employees in northern California. At the Victorian house, Bay says, there was an editing room in the basement, and the library and the dining room were offices. There were home-cooked family-style meals on Fridays and killer volleyball games on the lawn. (The sports tradition has continued at the Ranch. There is a softball diamond and a 150-player league and a completely equipped fitness center, including weights and aerobic rooms, racquetball and basketball courts, and a 25-meter pool.)

At the Victorian, Bay recalls, Lucas was already filling reams of yellow legal paper with sketches for the permanent place he had in

The Main House at Skywalker Ranch is outlined by lights in early evening. Designed by Lucas in a variety of Victorian styles and embodying his love of craftsmanship, it contains his offices and Lucasfilm's extensive research library.

The Technical Building (above), designed to look like an old brick winery, includes a vineyard on several acres next to the lake. Merlot, Chardonnay, and Pinot Noir wine is bottled each year for private use.

The Inn is part of the Ranch guest accommodations complex. Its exterior style is influenced by New England country farmhouses from the Victorian period. Directors, producers, editors, and writers live in the complex while working at the Ranch.

mind. "I've always been a frustrated architect," Lucas says, "and I like to build things. What I wanted to build was a work environment that is a model of the way I think creative people should be allowed to work."

With the money beginning to come in from both *American Graffiti* and *Star Wars*, in September 1978 he bought a 1,700-acre property called the Bulltail Ranch, fronting on Lucas Valley Road in Nicasio, California. Later Lucas bought several adjoining ranches, creating a total spread of some 6,000 acres, of which about 2,542 are part of the Skywalker Ranch master plan. With floor plans in hand, Lucas brought in professional architects to do the final blueprints. But the style of the buildings, their placement on the property, their floor plans, and their detailings, down to the doorknobs and light-switch panels, were all Lucas's, as was the overall concept of the place: the buildings should intrude upon the tranquil landscape as little as possible, should seem to have belonged to the land for a long time, and should be invisible from the highway, the building clusters even out of sight from each other. The majority of cars would be (and are) stashed in underground garages. All the utilities are also underground, combined in huge master conduits.

Construction on Skywalker Ranch began in early 1980. Jane Bay recalls that the first of what have become annual company picnics was held on the property in July 1979. As one of her jobs, Bay plans the picnic, which has included a marching band and, one year, rides in a hot-air balloon. The foundation of the Main House was poured in 1981, and a time capsule containing some *Star Wars* memorabilia—among them a letter from George's then-lawyer, Tom Pollock, confirming the go-ahead on the film—was buried.

As a help to the architects, Lucas devised a fanciful quick history for each of the buildings. The Main House, a large white mansion with a deep veranda, is in the Victorian style and dates from 1869, Lucas explained, with a library wing added in 1910. The head of the Ranch's mythical founding family added a gate house in 1870 and expanded it in 1915, when he also built a carriage house. The stable house dates from 1870, and the brook house (indeed built over a brook), which is designed in the Craftsman style Lucas frequently admired in houses in Berkeley, dates from 1913. The great brick winery is in fact the Technical Building, containing the recording stage and the state-of-the-art postproduction facilities. It is partly from 1880 but was extended and remodeled in the Art Moderne style in 1934 (possibly, although George does not say, when the winery went into production again after the repeal of Prohibition).

"The histories," Lucas explains, "helped everyone working on the project understand how they could have divergent styles side by side."

The most high tech of modern filmmakers has in fact a deep and abiding love for the patient and inspired craftsmanship of the American past, revealed at the Ranch in the exquisite paneling, much of it milled at the Ranch from first-growth redwood recycled from old railroad bridges, notably a wooden bridge that had been dismantled at Newport Beach, California. Some of that wood went into the magnificent spiral staircase in the library wing of the Main House. There is also an abundance of beautiful stained glass by a local artisan, Eric Christensen.

Organic gardener Brian Flannery is watering vegetable seedling flats in the Greenhouse, part of the Organic Garden. The produce is farmed year-round for use in the Ranch kitchens.

The interior of the Main House, where Lucas has his own suite of offices, is a mélange of Victorian styles—formal, informal, semiformal—with touches of the Art Nouveau, Mission, and Arts and Crafts styles.

"It was after *Star Wars* that I realized that I could actually build the ideal workplace," Lucas says. "The big Victorian house we had been living and working in was the embodiment of the idea that creative people need to work in pleasant circumstances and that it should be more homelike than businesslike."

Light, airiness, and a sense of the outdoors being only a pane away are very important to Lucas—needs born of his own work as an editor. "Editors!" Lucas exclaims. "In some places they're in windowless rooms ten hours a day. Having been an editor, I always thought that was wrong. People need to get out into the light and walk around and hear the birds sing. So this place was designed to give us all a sense that there's a world outside. For me, movies are made in the editing rooms. That's where I do the major part of my creative work, and it's extremely important to me that there be an atmosphere conducive to solving problems and coming up with good ideas."

A place less factory-like than Skywalker Ranch would be hard to imagine. Across from the winery/Technical Building now stand row on row of a flourishing vineyard. More than a thousand Merlot and Chardonnay vines were set out in 1987 and produced a first hundred-case bottling in 1992. This year another 3,300 vines were started on an additional three acres, with Pinot Noir vines added. The grapes are pressed and the wine made at Francis Coppola's winery a few miles away. The label reads "Vigne di Cielo Caminante" (Skywalker Wine).

Tom Forster, who joined Lucas in 1984 to organize the fire protection and security service, became the Ranch manager in 1989 and now oversees a staff of forty-five, including a well-equipped fire brigade that in emergencies also serves the surrounding community. Forster says proudly that as well as the vineyard there is a one-acre organic garden (about to be expanded to three acres). First planted in 1990 with advice from Alice Waters, an organic-foods enthusiast of the famous Chez Panisse restaurant in Berkeley, the garden supplies lettuce, tomatoes, broccoli, and other vegetables to the Ranch's three restaurants in the Main House, the Technical Building, and the new Fitness Center. "Over time we hope to be self-sufficient," Forster says, "even doing our own jams, jellies, and olive oil. We're not there yet, but we're getting there."

The Ranch is also home to a small herd of Texas longhorns, including cows, calves, a bull, and two trophy steers, and an ark's worth of other creatures—chickens, goats, a Jersey cow, rabbits, a burro, and six horses. Forster notes that the lawn clippings, kitchen

This beautiful stained-glass window in the Main House (above) was inspired by the work of Alphonse Mucha, a French poster artist working in the Art Nouveau period. The original design was completed in 1983 by Eric Christensen, with some improvements added in 1996 by Ian McCaig.

Lucas's love of craftsmanship is reflected in the pierced copper light fixtures and the handsome stained-glass "Shaker" window (the work of local artists Eric Christensen and Barry Reischman) in one of the guest suites on the Ranch (opposite).

scraps, and animal wastes are all composted to improve the soil.

Only 5 percent of Skywalker's land can be built on, Forster says, the rest having been deeded to an agricultural preserve. "George respects the land. He didn't want to create an impact greater than the equivalent impact of homes that could've been built under the existing zoning laws."

A later addition to the Ranch is an Archives Building, for storage of props, mattes, and models. For business guests and clients, Skywalker has a sumptuous suite of guest quarters, ranging from the size of a hotel room to three-bedroom apartments with kitchens, where filmmakers like Robert Redford and Brian De Palma have lived for months while overseeing postproduction on their films.

The Carl Larsson guest room in the Inn (top) was inspired by the style of the famous Swedish painter and illustrator. This apartment includes a living room, the sitting room as pictured, a bedroom, kitchenette, and dining alcove.

Italian film director Federico Fellini was the inspiration for this guest apartment (above) in the Bunk House, part of the Guest Complex. The accommodations include a comfortable bedroom, a spacious living room with a high ceiling, a kitchen, and a deck facing a beautiful wooded hillside.

The sun-filled solarium of the Main House (opposite) is climate-controlled by a system of automatic louvers. There are tables around its central garden where staffers can adjourn for lunch.

The walls at the Ranch, like the space above one of the several fireplaces in the Gate House, are hung with Lucas's collection of the work of the great illustrators. This painting is *The Swan* by Arthur Mathews, a San Francisco painter (above). Seen by moonlight, the Main House with its wide veranda suggests the home of a very large family rather than the headquarters of a very large enterprise.

One of the most impressive facilities at Skywalker is the research library, located in the Main House and launched by the now-retired Deborah Fine. She joined Lucas as a freelance researcher on *More American Graffiti* in 1978 and started compiling the library the next year. By now the library contains more than fifteen thousand volumes, has runs of two hundred periodicals (some dating back to the mid-nineteenth century), and a hundred file cabinets of pictures and texts. The collection incorporates a major film studio's entire research library, which Lucas bought a few years ago. There are now four librarians and an archivist who can come up with very nearly anything under the sun, from architecture to zoology, to help writers and production designers. With its glass-domed ceiling and the spiral staircase to its second level of shelves, the library is a beautiful space.

Gordon Radley, a Peace Corps veteran who became a lawyer and who is now president of Lucasfilm Ltd., says, "As a business-person, coming out of Los Angeles, I thought the isolation of the Ranch would drive me crazy. On the contrary, I love it. There's a lack of noise, a lack of disruption, a lack of distraction. It enhances your focus. You don't run out and do errands at lunch, so you really feel part of a common endeavor."

The Ranch reminds Radley of the secluded atmosphere of a very good, small liberal arts college. "There is an academic tradition that the quest for truth or art needs to be apart from society, from the trappings of daily life. . . . George understood that and wanted to enhance the experience by allowing creativity to emerge free of stress and distraction."

The Ranch fully reflects George's remarkable and successful blend of risk taker and traditionalist (in terms of personal taste). As in the matter of his bold investments in digital technology, he has sometimes gone against the advice of cautious colleagues. He was advised to hold off on the Technical Building's excellent large recording stage, which is now usually booked a year in advance. John Williams, who did the original *Star Wars* music (and many other scores, for both Lucas and Steven Spielberg), calls the stage "fantastic." "We did some recordings with what George calls the 'Skywalker Symphony,' which is made up of symphony players and faculty members from around the Bay Area. It's something George is like a child about. He comes to the sessions. He had T-shirts made for the players."

The concept of Skywalker Ranch as a kind of superbly equipped filmmakers' retreat has been changed by the explosive growth of Lucasfilm itself. Jane Bay has said that only two years after she was one of four Lucas staffers in Marin County, there were three hundred. Yet as filmmakers come to Skywalker to do postproduction on their films, or spend time at Industrial Light & Magic in San Rafael consulting on visual effects, that original dream of a filmmakers' commune (far from Hollywood) is in a real if somewhat altered sense coming true.

Skywalker Ranch is not yet complete, and Lucas is still making sketches on yellow pads. Under a recent agreement with Marin County, there will be a new adjoining master-planned development for digital production and multimedia work, tucked away in the hills, unseen from the highway, looking to the future.

Explaining his risk-taking investments, George Lucas says with a laugh, "Sometimes visionaries are a little ahead of their time. But you'd be wise to listen to them. Sometimes they're right."

The stunning two-level library centers on the spiral staircase, carved from ancient redwood from an abandoned bridge. The stained-glass dome was, like the windows, designed by Eric Christensen.

In his undergraduate days, Lucas dreamed of being an experimental filmmaker based in San Francisco, a guerrilla documentarian, as he once said. Later on, he also dreamed of having a state-of-the-art production facility, where he and other filmmakers could work totally removed from the pressures of Hollywood. The successes, first of *American Graffiti* and then, overwhelmingly, of *Star Wars,* altered his dreams dramatically in size and complexity.

From its beginnings in the early 1970s, the enterprise Lucas launched as Lucasfilm Ltd. has grown by tremendous leaps, fired by the ongoing popularity of *Star Wars* merchandise, by the huge expansion of Industrial Light & Magic and its domination of the special effects and computer graphics fields, and by the worldwide popularity of LucasArts' interactive products.

Coping with the administrative challenge of this growth, Lucas found that he was very busy being a corporate executive, at the expense of the time he preferred to spend as a creative filmmaker, editor, and producer. To meet the ongoing challenge, in 1989 Lucas formed a subsidiary to contain all of his nonfilmmaking business activities, allowing him to focus on what he likes to do best: film production. When the advancement of digital technology began to accelerate in the early 1990s, Lucas foresaw the impact it would have on the entertainment industry, and in 1993 he restructured the organization into three companies—Lucasfilm Ltd., Lucas Digital Ltd., and LucasArts Entertainment Company—in order to provide for greater management flexibility and to take advantage of new corporate opportunities.

Lucasfilm Ltd. is the parent company. It embraces all of Lucas's film and television production and distribution, and is one of the

Sculpting a villain, an ILM model maker (right) creates a head that will undergo indignities no actor would allow.

A meticulously detailed scale-model house (opposite), divided by the evil forces in *Jumanji*, gets final touches from one of ILM's wizards of miniature-making.

most successful independent production companies in the world, with at last count forty-four Academy Award nominations that led to seventeen Oscars for its features. Its president is Gordon Radley, a Peace Corps veteran and lawyer who joined Lucas in 1985.

"The wonderful thing," says Radley, "is that each new year is more successful than the last in both top-line and bottom-line terms. One of George's dreams has been that the company should be able to succeed without his direct involvement. And what he enjoys now is that the businesses are all self-sustaining and profitable."

Most recently, Lucas has formed Lucas Learning, a new venture born of his long-standing belief in the educational possibilities of interactive multimedia programs. Susan Schilling, a twenty-year veteran of the field, heads up Lucas Learning.

THE THX GROUP

Within Lucasfilm Ltd. is the THX Group, headed by Monica L. Dashwood. THX is dedicated to improving the quality of motion picture sound and images as they are presented not only in theaters but also in home theater environments. The THX trailer, "The Audience Is Listening," is now seen and heard in more than fourteen hundred cinemas here and abroad.

The division took shape in 1982 when Lucas hired Tomlinson Holman, a leading audio engineer, to build a state-of-the-art post-production facility for the making of *Return of the Jedi*. After examining the whole process of film sound, from recording on the set to playback in the theater, Holman and Lucasfilm engineers created a proprietary system that incorporates a unique combination of loudspeakers, integrated with the acoustics of specific spaces, that affect the actual design and construction of the theater. There are THX theaters and mixing rooms in more than twenty-four countries.

The proprietary technology developed over the years by Home THX is now licensed to more than fifty manufacturers of high-performance audio components that go into THX Home Theater Systems. The THX systems allow the intentions of the filmmakers to be reproduced at home in full-spectrum, undistorted volume and multi-speaker, wraparound sound—a thrilling improvement on the traditional flat, frontal living-room audio.

In addition, through its Digital Mastering Program, THX helps filmmakers ensure the best possible transfer of their movies to laser discs, videotapes, and DVD. THX creates video masters with such added features as closed captioning and chapter search. The group also has a patented Vertical Interval Test Signal, which is added to the video master and provides a point of reference and constant check on several elements that affect viewing quality, including frequency response and color saturation. In addition to ensuring exact reproduction of the picture, the THX engineers also ascertain that the digital sound tracks are indistinguishable from the originals. The quality assurance on laser discs includes frequent checks during the actual stamping of the discs.

The same close overseeing of the transfers from film to laser disc takes place in the creation of master tapes for videocassettes. The program made its debut with the videocassette release of the *Star Wars* trilogy in the fall of 1995.

The THX logo is already familiar on laser discs and videocassettes, as it is in cinemas, and indications are that laser discs bearing the THX logos outsell those without it.

THX also maintains a Theater Alignment Program (TAP), which checks release prints for filmmakers and studios, aligns projection and sound equipment at theaters (whether they are THX theaters or not), and makes random evaluations during performances.

LUCASFILM LICENSING

The highly successful Lucasfilm Licensing operation is run by Howard Roffman, a lawyer, photographer, and seventeen-year Lucas veteran. Under Roffman, Licensing has overseen the development (and carefully monitored the quality) of an extraordinary range of publications, toys, and innumerable other *Star Wars*–themed products.

The *Star Wars* novels, further extensions of the saga, often written by well-known science-fiction and fantasy authors, have consistently made the *New York Times* best-seller lists. In early 1996, Lucasfilm Licensing launched a major new *Star Wars* episode called *Shadows of the Empire*, set between *The Empire Strikes Back* and *Return of the Jedi*. It was a multimedia event: not only was there a novel (by Steve Perry) but also a six-part comic book series, an enhanced sound track CD, a series of toys (a Micro Machine collection and action figures), and a new interactive console game from LucasArts for the Nintendo 64 format.

The amazing merchandise includes such items as a set of metal cards featuring Ralph McQuarrie's legendary *Star Wars* art, a life-size latex reproduction of Yoda, bank checks with *Star Wars* scenes, and even a *Star Wars* version of the popular board game "Monopoly."

The toys are consistently best-sellers, and also prizewinners. In 1995, *Action Figure News and Toy Review* gave *Star Wars*–themed toys four bests, including one for the Star Wars Electronic Talking Bank. Another, for best miniatures, went to the Star Wars Action Fleet.

"The most important strategic decision George ever made," Roffman says, "was to retain the sequel rights to the *Star Wars* property. When it came to doing *The Empire Strikes Back,* he had the leverage to get back the merchandising rights. I think his idea was simply to maintain creative integrity. Who could imagine that twenty years later *Star Wars* would be one of the most important licensing properties in history?"

Roffman adds, "All the licensed products are just extensions of what *Star Wars* means to the audience, and it's important to have control of what gets put out there, how it looks, and how it's done.

"*Star Wars* is a cherished part of the culture," Roffman says, "and we're in the *Star Wars* business for the long term."

The continuing appeal of the saga is borne out by the fact that Pepsico recently signed a promotional arrangement for *Star Wars* that is unprecedented in size and scope. For the first time in history, promotional programs for restaurants, beverages, and snack food will be united around the world behind a single entertainment property: *Star Wars.*

A small sampling of *Star Wars* merchandise includes action figures, books, CD-ROM games, and a life-size Yoda. Guarding a heritage, Lucasfilm Licensing keeps tight control on quality and taste.

LUCAS DIGITAL LTD.

The title of the company—Lucas Digital Ltd.—reflects the revolutionary shift to digital technology in filmmaking that Lucas first envisioned years ago and, often in the face of skepticism from the industry, made a reality. The company has two divisions, Industrial Light & Magic (ILM) and Skywalker Sound.

"Lucas Digital," says Lucas, "is what one would describe as our production service company."

The company is headed by Jim Morris, who joined ILM in 1987 as a visual-effects producer and worked on *The Abyss*, among other films.

INDUSTRIAL LIGHT & MAGIC

Industrial Light & Magic began life in 1975 in a warehouse in Van Nuys, California, to produce the visual effects for *Star Wars*—which largely meant inventing the technology to create them. Three years later, ILM moved to its present location in San Rafael, California, to do the effects for *The Empire Strikes Back* and *Return of the Jedi*.

Over the years since, ILM has gone from being a traditional visual-effects company to becoming the largest all-digital production company in the world. "We're focusing more on animation and 3-D computer animation and less on the more generic special effects we did in the past," Lucas says.

"We're in a digital revolution," Jim Morris adds. "A lot of the traditional processes that were photochemical before are digital now—optical compositing, miniature construction, and photography. We still create miniatures, but instead of creating them in physical space, we create virtual models and essentially photograph them inside the computer."

ILM has grown in size threefold in five years, Morris says, and all the work is completed using digital technology.

"To put it all in context," Morris adds, "we have developed the technology here, but George has envisioned the technology that should be developed."

Lucas recalls, "In the process of building up the computer technology for ILM to become a completely digital special-effects company, we created a computer division. The division, which developed the EditDroid, also developed the Pixar high-speed graphics computer, which we spun off to Steve Jobs of Apple Computers once we had the technology. That was a company we developed here for ten years. Pixar went on to fame and fortune, making *Toy Story*. But the $50 million that Jobs had to spend to develop the company fully, I decided to invest in multimedia, in the games division. We already had a production company."

ILM currently works on a dozen major films a year and perhaps four dozen large-scale commercials. Among its recent achievements have been the first use of digital technology to create a photo-real living character with skin, muscles, and texture (in *Jurassic Park*), the first computer-generated animals with hair and fur (for *Jumanji*), and the first fully synthetic speaking characters with distinct personalities and emotions (for *Casper*). The company has also worked on *Twister, Forrest Gump, Dragonheart* (creating the delicious dragon voiced by Sean Connery), and *The Lost World*, the sequel to *Jurassic Park*. In all, ILM has worked on more than one hundred films and won fourteen Academy Awards for Best Achievement in Visual Effects. Not less significantly, ILM has won nine Technical Achievement Awards from the Academy for innovative techniques and processes.

"I had the pleasure of picking up one of these awards recently, for digital compositing," says Jim Morris. "Interestingly, as the other companies got up to accept their awards, they thanked George for envisioning that we should be able to do these things in the first place."

At ILM model maker Larry Tan (opposite) works on a mock-up of the Death Star. Lucas looks at the final model.

A giant eye (right) destined to be in a 3M commercial—another part of ILM's output—takes shape as a model maker tends to the lashes.

Baby dinosaurs for Steven Spielberg's *Jurassic Park* get finishing touches, assembly-line style, from another of ILM's magicians (below).

A matte artist paints a scenic background for Spielberg's *Hook* in 1991 (top). Digital technology is now changing the nature of matte work.

Detailing a cathedral-sized model house for the 1992 black comedy *Death Becomes Her* requires three ILM miniaturists (above).

A scale-model mountain range (opposite) is created as the setting for the Andes plane crash in Frank Marshall's 1993 film *Alive!*.

Taking flight at ILM (overleaf), one of the Fairies in *Willow* hangs in space for a special-effects shot watched by effects supervisor Dennis Muren (arms folded) and Lucas.

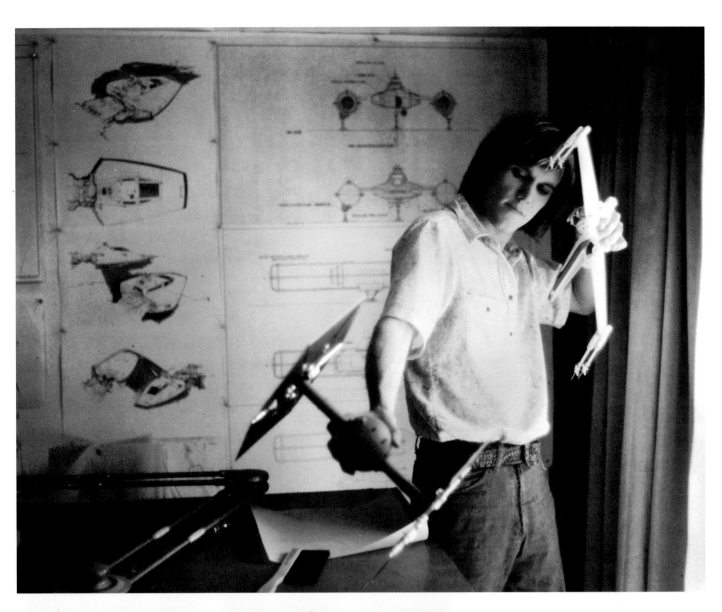

Joe Johnston (above), an ILM designer who later directed *The Rocketeer*, checks perspectives on the Tie fighter and X-wing for *Star Wars*.

Matte painters (left) can now paint electronically directly on screen in the special-effects world of computer graphics, which ILM has pioneered.

Maneuvering the dreaded, two-headed Eborsisk monster from *Willow*, an ILM artist makes the minute adjustments that will, in stop-motion animation, bring the Eborsisk to life (opposite).

SKYWALKER SOUND

The building has been designed to resemble a turn-of-the-century winery, set in a fold of the Marin County hills at Skywalker Ranch. But, in fact, the 145,000-square-foot interior is the home of Skywalker Sound, with its six mixing studios, a world-class recording stage, a variety of sound- and picture-editing rooms, a superb theater, and other facilities. The complex is one of the largest and most versatile postproduction facilities in the world and reflects Lucas's long-standing dream of totally digital postproduction editing.

"We've been working for fifteen years to develop a completely unified system for postproduction," Lucas says. From the effort came EditDroid and SoundDroid, developed in 1982, and one of the first electronic nonlinear editing systems ever created. These systems have since been sold to Avid Technologies, although the Lucas companies and Avid continue to work together on later, even more skillful, generations of the systems.

"Skywalker has gone all digital," says Lucas. "The idea is to have a completely digital postproduction system. Once you shoot the film, it goes in the system and becomes digital and you finish it digitally." (The perfected digital copy is then converted back to film.) "There are rudimentary versions now; and we're working toward a more sophisticated version."

Thanks to digital tie-lines utilizing fiber-optic cables capable of carrying six-track sound recordings, it is no longer necessary for producers to come to Skywalker Ranch to view or hear work in progress. "We can put in 'phone booths,'" Lucas says, "a little THX screening room, wherever the producers are—Los Angeles, Chicago, Connecticut. We can let them see the picture, the effects, the sound, all with no loss of quality. And as they watch, we can have conversations with them, work on the film with them. It's a phone call."

Skywalker Sound, says Jim Morris, has provided sound for more than half of the twenty-five top-grossing films of all time. These include *E.T., Raiders of the Lost Ark, The Empire Strikes Back, Return of the Jedi, Terminator 2,* and *Forrest Gump.*

It has had many Academy Award nominations, and ten Oscars for Best Achievement in Sound and Sound Effects Editing. More recently it has added Clios and other industry awards for its commercials.

Mixing the sound for a scene from *Jurassic Park,* Gary Rydstrom works the controls at an elaborate console at Skywalker Sound.

Composer David Michael Frank conducts the orchestra for the IMAX film *Cosmic Voyage* on Skywalker Sound's state-of-the-art recording stage (opposite).

LUCASARTS ENTERTAINMENT COMPANY

What is now LucasArts Entertainment Company began as Lucasfilm Games, which was born of Lucas's fascination with the uses of interactive multimedia. Beyond its demonstrated popularity for elaborate and fun games, Lucas foresaw the usefulness of the technology as an educational tool. But the games proved to have a life of their own. Today the renamed LucasArts Entertainment Company stands second in the computer games market.

The games specifically inspired by *Star Wars*, most recently including *Rebel Assault,* alone have sold nearly 3 million copies worldwide—far and away a record for any such series.

Founded in 1982 and now run by Jack Sorensen, LucasArts was the first games developer and publisher to be fully integrated with a film company. What this gave LucasArts from the beginning was a rich heritage of film experience, so that its games have always featured compelling storytelling, careful attention to character development, and vivid settings, plus the George Lucas tradition of being on the cutting edge of visual and sound effects. The games feature 3-D animation, live-action video, and interactive digital sound, and they are produced in several different computer formats to serve various markets. The games importantly stress "gameplay"—interactivity between the player and the story that not only demands agility but confronts the player with a variety of choices, lending additional challenges and excitement to the game.

LucasArts now has nearly 250 employees, and 70 percent of them are involved in game development. Their talents are diverse: fine arts, traditional animation, graphic design, architecture, and video production. The company has expanded the boundaries of 2-D animation, 3-D graphics, the capture of motion, and live action in electronic gaming.

LucasArts has developed much of its own software—often with titles almost as provocative as the games. iMUSE (for Interactive Music and Sound Effects) lets sound respond instantly to the players' unpredictable choices. The "engines" to drive the games include SCUMM (Script Creation Utility for *Maniac Mansion,* the company's best-selling 1987 game) and INSANE (INteractive Streaming and ANimation Engine).

The library now includes seventeen titles based on *Star Wars* and *Indiana Jones* and twenty-six original-concept games. *Rebel Assault,* launched in 1993, has sold more than 1.5 million copies; *X-Wing* and *Dark Forces* have sold nearly as well. The best-selling original titles have been *The Dig* and *Full Throttle.* The top twelve LucasArts games are described here.

The games are sold in thirty countries in twelve languages and to date have earned more than 150 industry awards. As evidence of the popularity of the games, the company's Web site—www.lucasarts.com—receives more than a million hits a month.

THE GAMES

Ballblazer (1985)
One of the first half-dozen games developed by LucasArts Entertainment, *Ballblazer* (above) was, like the others, created for publication and distribution by other companies. It set a new, high standard in multiplayer gaming. Players operated hoverlike craft to play a kind of futuristic Rugby, the object being to get a fiery orb to the opponent's goal. It was so popular in Atari and Commodore 64 formats that it left no doubt the company was destined to establish its own brand of premier game products, publishing, distributing, and marketing to the growing base of game players. In 1996, *Ballblazer* itself was redesigned to take advantage of new technology, including creation of a real-time 3-D environment, for the Sony Playstation. It is now a game for multiple players competing in the Interstellar Ballblazer Championship on an artificial asteroid.

Maniac Mansion (1987)
Produced originally in 1987 for the Commodore and Apple personal computers, *Maniac Mansion* (opposite above) was called a breakthrough in game design. Described as a zany cross between *Rocky Horror Picture Show* and *The Addams Family*, it was such a roaring success that in 1989 it was upgraded for the IBM, Amiga, and Atari systems, with enhanced sound effects, high-resolution graphics, and

What are you doing!!!

Walk to

Push   Open   Walk to   Unlock   Turn
Pull   Close   Pick up   Turn
Give   Read   What is   Use   Fix

search for the Holy Grail. It was launched just two weeks after the movie's release, and the team at LucasArts had full access to the scripts, set designs, and even the props of the film, all heightening the cinematic "feel" of the game. A unique feature lets players select dialogue for Indy to say—sarcastic or charming, for example—and the choices affect the plot. Player scores are measured by an I.Q. ("Indy Quotient"), earned by finding subtle solutions to Indy's problems. A sixty-four-page "Grail Diary," kept by Indy's father, Henry, and supplied with the game, is a treasury of useful clues, and shrewd game players can find ploys the movies overlooked.

detailed animation. Shortly after, the game was redone for the popular Nintendo Entertainment System and used as the inspiration for a syndicated television series of the same name. In the game, a mad scientist and his weirdo associates capture a pretty cheerleader and prepare her for irreversible brain surgery. Players can pick among fourteen different three-person rescue teams, leading to five different endings. The game involves only a mouse or joystick, no keyboarding. There are delicious sight gags and all the hallmarks of the Lucasfilm approach, including tracking shots (horizontal scrolling), cutaways to action elsewhere ("Meanwhile, back at the ranch"), and notably detailed and convincing graphics.

Give   Pick up   Use
Open   Talk to   Push
Close   Look at   Pull

Indiana Jones and the Fate of Atlantis (1992)
Set in the 1930s, the game has Indy and his cohort Sophia Hapgood racing the Nazis to find the potent magic of the Lost City of Atlantis —magic that may help create the atomic bomb that both Germany and the United States are trying to build. *Fate of Atlantis* (above) was the largest and most complex game Lucas had yet published, with more than 200 "rooms" and 100 pieces of original background art, all in 256 colors, and with 40 characters speaking 8,000 lines of dialogue. ("It took four weeks to record the speech," noted producer-director Tamlynn Barra.) The game's ingenious structure included three different playing "paths," plus additional complex puzzles with alternative solutions, making *Fate of Atlantis* almost infinitely replayable. Players also get to control a German submarine, steer a hot-air balloon, and operate a mysterious Atlantissian machine.

Walk to
Push   Open   Walk to   Use   Talk
Pull   Close   Pick up   **Turn on**   Fight
Give   Look   What is   Turn off

Indiana Jones and the Last Crusade: The Graphic Adventure (1989)
Inspired by the blockbuster film produced by Lucasfilm, Ltd., *The Graphic Adventure* (above) is, like the movie, built around Indy's

X-Wing (1993)

X-Wing (above) was the best-selling personal computer game of the year—so popular that it was significantly enhanced and released in 1994 as a CD-ROM, along with two subsequent game episodes, *Imperial Pursuit* and *B-Wing*, in a package called *X-Wing Collector's CD*. In its maiden flight, *X-Wing* was the first PC product to draw players into the *Star Wars* universe. The CD-ROM version added six new combat missions, bringing the total to 122, as the Rebel Alliance pilots seek to destroy Darth Vader's Imperial Forces. Lucas model designers upgraded the X-wings, A-wings, and B-wings the players fly. Added, too, are one thousand lines of mission briefings. Thanks to improved stereo sound, the Tie fighters zoom across the screen in remarkably realistic sonic 3-D. The later episodes follow the destruction of the Death Star and the search for a new Rebel base.

Rebel Assault (1993)

With *Rebel Assault* (above) and its homage to *Star Wars*, LucasArts set out to create a new standard for CD-ROM entertainment, with a combination of a terrific story, newly challenging interactivity for the player, and a dazzling array of technical achievements. "We immersed the players in the *Star Wars* universe," said project manager Vince Lee. There is in fact footage from *Star Wars* as well as new video footage, and the sound track includes John Williams's majestic theme from the movies, performed by the London Symphony. The game sequences are remarkably realistic, thanks to advanced 3-D modeling techniques (used throughout the entire game for the first time). The hero is Rookie One, a young Rebel pilot, and players can make Rookie One male or female, with the program providing the appropriate voice and physique. The game can be played at three levels of difficulty to match the gamesters' skills, and Rookie One progresses from training flights to the famous trench run on the Death Star in an X-wing.

Dark Forces (1995)

A new *Star Wars* story featuring Rebel special agent Kyle Katarn, *Dark Forces* (above) is a first-person action-adventure. Players navigate through more than a dozen complex, realistic, multilevel CD environments and control the firepower of a whole arsenal of weapons—blasters, ion guns, thermal detonators, assault rifles—to destroy the Empire's Dark Trooper. Katarn is extremely mobile, with the ability to rotate 360 degrees, jump and crouch, and look all around. The environments are highly animated, with such perils as ceiling-mounted rifles and flowing rivers. Faced with all these challenges, players can set the game's degree of difficulty from beginner to advanced. Some of the "worlds" reflect locations from the *Star Wars* trilogy. But other planets and spacecraft were created specially for the game.

Full Throttle (1995)

In a futuristic world, motorcycle gangs battle furiously in the dark adventure *Full Throttle* (above). Ben, the heroic leader of one of the gangs, the Polecats, has to clear himself of a murder charge, find the real murderer, win over a doubting heiress, and prevent the destruction of the beloved Corley Motors, whose bikes rule the road. The digital "engine" that powered the action in *Rebel Assault* is used for first-person thrills in *Full Throttle*. The game features the most extensive compositing to date of 3-D graphics and animation and has an all-digital sound track. The cycles are dazzling in their custom detailing, and the fights among the four rival gangs are extraordinarily vivid and thrilling. Among its several awards, *Full Throttle* was named Best Adventure game of the year by *Computer Player* magazine.

The Dig (1995)

Inspired by Steven Spielberg's vision of a game that would combine the feel of *Forbidden Planet* and the human psychology of *The Treasure of the Sierra Madre,* top science-fiction writer Orson Scott Card and project leader Sean Clark created a uniquely dramatic story about a team of space explorers stranded on an alien planet (above). ILM created amazing special effects—spaceships, asteroids, and planets moving in space, and eerily atmospheric backgrounds melding 3-D and 2-D effects. In this world, an asteroid proves to be an alien spaceship inhabited by a race that has discovered immortality—but desperately needs something from their earthling captives. The characters (Commander Boston Low, geologist Ludger Brink, and journalist Maggie Robbins) and their relationships are so complex and interesting that a novelization, an audio version, and a CD sound track were issued simultaneously. It became LucasArts' best-selling adventure game at that time and received critical acclaim from leading magazine game reviewers. The remarkable sound track uses LucasArts' patented system, Interactive Music and Sound Effects, or iMUSE.

Rebel Assault II: The Hidden Empire (1995)

Like the original *Rebel Assault* (more than 1.5 million copies sold worldwide), *Rebel Assault II* (above) is set in the *Star Wars* universe, with an original story and live-action video. The stars, Rookie One and Ru Murleen, animated in the original *Rebel*, are now played by professional actors in authentic costumes and set against computer-generated 3-D backgrounds. It is one of the few times George Lucas has allowed filming of a *Star Wars* fantasy. The action-arcade game features improved game play and a technologically advanced "engine" to propel the game. Rookie One, investigating a kind of galactic Bermuda Triangle and discovering a new Imperial plot against the Rebel Alliance, is called on to pilot starfighters, a speeder bike, and even a Millennium Falcon–type transport. For the player, good aim and quick reflexes are still vital, but Rookie One also has to be adroit at dodging behind shields to avoid stormtrooper fire. As well as the improved graphics, *Rebel Assault II* has stereo surround sound and rich color.

Afterlife (1996)

Possibly the wildest and farthest out, galactically speaking, of the Lucas games is *Afterlife* (above). Created by Michael Stemmle, *Afterlife* puts players in charge of building and managing Heaven and Hell on an alien planet. For LucasArts it represented a new genre of games—the strategic simulation of life scenarios. It's not exactly real life here, what with Aria Goodhalo guiding players around Heaven and keeping score, and Jasper Wormsworth doing the same for the Other Place. The perils to thwart the players include Heaven Nose, Hell in a Handbasket, and, of course, Hell Freezes Over. The graphics for both places are brilliantly surrealistic; seldom do games so successfully meld excitement, amusement, and verbal delight. *Afterlife* features more than 250 intricately detailed settings and structures, and many graphs and statistics.

Mortimer and the Riddles of the Medallion (1996)

The first game LucasArts Entertainment created especially for children in the four-to-nine age group, *Mortimer* (below) is an exciting fantasy about an evil doctor who has frozen all the animals in the world into statues. Only Sid, Sally, and Mortimer (a giant snail) can unfreeze them by quickly reassembling the pieces of a magic medallion. There are riddles to be solved and a chance for youngsters to learn about animals (fulfilling George Lucas's dream that multimedia games can be educational too). Collette Michaud, who was the project leader, says, "I've always fantasized about flying," and, thanks to 3-D graphics and 2-D animation techniques developed for *Rebel Assault*, the children zoom through a virtual world.

FILMOGRAPHY

STUDENT FILMS AND SHORT FILMS

Look at Life (1965)
George Lucas's first film, one minute long, made for a USC class in animation.

Herbie (1966)
Codirected by George Lucas and Paul Golding, as an exercise for a USC class in cinematic design.

1.42.08 (1966)
Written and directed by George Lucas.

The Emperor (1967)
Documentary of a Los Angeles disc jockey, directed by George Lucas.

THX 1138:4EB (Electronic Labyrinth) (1967)
Written and directed by George Lucas.

Anyone Lived in a Pretty How Town (1967)
Directed by George Lucas; written by George Lucas and Paul Golding.

6.18.67 (1967)
Conceived and directed by George Lucas; documentary relating to the making of Carl Foreman's *McKenna's Gold*.

Filmmaker (1968)
Documentary about Francis Ford Coppola, written, directed, photographed, and edited by George Lucas.

FEATURES

THX 1138 (Released March 11, 1971)

An American Zoetrope Production
A Warner Brothers release
Executive produced by Francis Coppola
Produced by Lawrence Sturhahn
Directed by George Lucas
Screenplay by George Lucas and Walter Murch, based on a story by George Lucas
Edited by George Lucas
Art direction by Michael Haller
Photography by Dave Meyers and Albert Kihn
Music by Lalo Schifrin
Sound by Walter Murch, Louis Yates, Jim Manson

Featuring: Robert Duvall, Donald Pleasence, Don Pedro Colley, Maggie McOmie, Ian Wolfe

American Graffiti (Released August 1, 1973)

A Lucasfilm Ltd./Coppola Company Production
A Universal Pictures release

Produced by Francis Coppola
Coproduced by Gary Kurtz
Directed by George Lucas
Screenplay by George Lucas, Gloria Katz, and Willard Huyck
Edited by Verna Fields and Marcia Lucas
Art direction by Dennis Clark
Visual Consultant: Haskell Wexler
Directors of Photography: Ron Eveslage and Jan D'Alquen
Sound montage and rerecording by Walter Murch
Costume design by Aggie Guerard Rodgers

Featuring: Richard Dreyfuss, Ron Howard, Paul Le Mat, Charlie Martin Smith, Cindy Williams, Candy Clark, McKenzie Phillips, Wolfman Jack, Harrison Ford, Bo Hopkins, Manuela Padilla, Jr., Bo Gentry
Academy Award nominations: best picture, best director, best original story and screenplay, best film editing, best supporting actress (Candy Clark)

Star Wars (Released May 25, 1977)

A Lucasfilm Ltd. Production
A 20th Century-Fox release
Produced by Gary Kurtz
Written and directed by George Lucas
Edited by Paul Hirsch, Marcia Lucas, and Richard Chew
Production design by John Barry
Photography by Gilbert Taylor, B.S.C.
Music by John Williams
Special dialogue and sound-effects by Ben Burtt
Special Photographic Effects Supervisor: John Dykstra
Costume design by John Mollo

Featuring: Mark Hamill, Harrison Ford, Carrie Fisher, Alec Guinness, Anthony Daniels, Peter Mayhew, Kenny Baker, Peter Cushing, David Prowse
Academy Awards: best original score, best film editing, best sound, best art and set decoration, best costume design, best visual effects
Special Achievement Academy Award: sound-effects creations
Academy Award nominations: best picture, best original story and screenplay, best director, best supporting actor (Alec Guinness)

More American Graffiti (Released August 3, 1979)

A Lucasfilm Ltd. Production
A Universal Pictures release
Executive produced by George Lucas
Produced by Howard Kazanjian
Written and directed by B. W. L. Norton, based on characters created by George Lucas, Gloria Katz, and Willard Huyck
Edited by Tina Hirsch
Art direction by Ray Storey
Director of Photography: Caleb Deschanel
Costume design by Aggie Guerard Rodgers

Featuring: Candy Clark, Bo Hopkins, Ron Howard, Cindy Williams, Paul Le Mat, McKenzie Phillips, Charlie Martin Smith

The Empire Strikes Back (Released May 21, 1980)

A Lucasfilm Ltd. Production
A 20th Century-Fox release
Executive produced by George Lucas
Produced by Gary Kurtz
Directed by Irvin Kershner
Screenplay by Leigh Brackett and Lawrence Kasdan, from a story by George Lucas
Edited by Paul Hirsch, A.C.E.
Production design by Norman Reynolds
Director of Photography: Peter Suschitzsky, B.S.C.
Music by John Williams
Sound design by Ben Burtt
Special visual effects by Brian Johnson and Richard Edlund, A.S.C.
Costume design by John Mollo

Featuring: Mark Hamill, Harrison Ford, Carrie Fisher, Billy Dee Williams, Alec Guinness, Anthony Daniels, Kenny Baker, Peter Mayhew, Frank Oz, David Prowse
Academy Award: best sound
Special Achievement Academy Award: visual effects
Academy Award nominations: best art direction and set decoration, best original score

Raiders of the Lost Ark (Released June 12, 1981)

A Lucasfilm Ltd. Production
A Paramount Pictures release
Executive produced by George Lucas and Howard Kazanjian
Produced by Frank Marshall
Directed by Steven Spielberg
Screenplay by Lawrence Kasdan, from a story by George Lucas and Philip Kaufman
Edited by Michael Kahn, A.C.E.
Production design by Norman Reynolds
Director of Photography: Douglas Slocombe
Music by John Williams
Sound design by Ben Burtt
Visual Effects Supervisor: Richard Edlund, A.S.C.
Costume design by Deborah Nadoolman

Featuring: Harrison Ford, Karen Allen, John Rhys-Davies, Denholm Elliott, Paul Freeman, Ronald Lacey
Academy Awards: best art direction, best sound, best film editing, best visual effects
Special Achievement Academy Award: sound-effects editing
Academy Award nominations: best picture, best director, best cinematography, best original score

Twice Upon a Time (Released August 1982) Animation

A Korty Films and Lucasfilm Ltd. Presentation
A Ladd Company Production
A Warner Brothers release
Executive produced by George Lucas
Produced by Bill Couturie

Produced and directed by John Korty and Charles Swenson
Screenplay by John Korty, Charles Swenson, Suella Kennedy, Bill Couturie
Story by John Korty, Bill Couturie, Suella Kennedy
Edited by Jennifer Gallagher
Art direction by Harley Jessup
Music by Dawn Atkinson and Ken Melville
Sound design by Walt Kraemer

Featuring the voices of Marshall Efron, Hamilton Camp, Paul Frees, Judith
    Kahan Kampmann, James Cranna, Julie Payne

Return of the Jedi (Released May 25, 1983)

A Lucasfilm Ltd. Production
A 20th Century-Fox release
Executive produced by George Lucas
Produced by Howard Kazanjian
Directed by Richard Marquand
Screenplay by Lawrence Kasdan and George Lucas, from a story by George Lucas
Edited by Sean Barton, Marcia Lucas, and Duwayne Dunham
Production design by Norman Reynolds
Director of Photography: Alan Hume, B.S.C.
Music by John Williams
Sound design by Ben Burtt
Visual effects by Richard Edlund, A.S.C., Dennis Muren, Ken Ralston
Costume design by Aggie Guerard Rodgers and Nilo Rodis-Jamero

Featuring: Harrison Ford, Mark Hamill, Carrie Fisher, Billy Dee Williams,
    Anthony Daniels, Peter Mayhew, Alec Guinness, James Earl Jones,
    Sebastian Shaw, Ian McDiarmid, Frank Oz, David Prowse
Special Achievement Academy Award: visual effects
Academy Award nominations: best art direction and set decoration, best
    sound-effects editing, best original score, best sound

Indiana Jones and the Temple of Doom (Released May 23, 1984)

A Lucasfilm Ltd. Production
A Paramount Pictures release
Executive produced by George Lucas and Frank Marshall
Produced by Robert Watts
Directed by Steven Spielberg
Screenplay by Willard Huyck and Gloria Katz, based on a story by George Lucas
Edited by Michael Kahn, A.C.E.
Production design by Eliot Scott
Director of Photography: Douglas Slocombe
Music by John Williams
Sound design by Ben Burtt
Visual Effects Supervisor: Dennis Muren
Costume design by Anthony Powell

Featuring: Harrison Ford, Kate Capshaw, Ke Huy Quan, Philip Stone, Amrish
    Puri, Roshan Seth
Academy Award: best visual effects
Academy Award nomination: best original score

Mishima (Released September 1985)

A Francis Ford Coppola and George Lucas Presentation
A Zoetrope Studios/Filmlink Intl. (Tokyo)/Lucasfilm Ltd. Production
A Warner Brothers release
Executive produced by George Lucas and Francis Coppola
Directed by Paul Schrader
Screenplay by Paula and Leonard Schrader
Edited by Michael Chandler
Production design by Eiko Ishioka
Director of Photography: John Bailey
Music by Philip Glass
Sound design by Leslie Shatz
Costume design by Etsuko Yagyu

Featuring: Ken Ogata, Ken Sawada, Yasosuke Bando, Masayuki Shionoya,
    Toshi Yuki Nagashima

Latino (Released February 1986)

A Lucasfilm Ltd. Presentation
A Cinecom International release
Produced by Benjamin Berg
Directed by Haskell Wexler
Screenplay by Haskell Wexler
Edited by Robert Dalva
Director of Photography: Tom Sigel
Music by Diane Louie

Featuring: Robert Beltran, Annette Cardona, Tony Plana

Labyrinth (Released June 27, 1986)

A Henson Associates and Lucasfilm Ltd. Presentation
A Tri-Star release
Executive produced by George Lucas
Produced by Eric Rattray
Directed by Jim Henson
Screenplay by Terry Jones, from a story by Dennis Less and Jim Henson
Edited by John Grover
Production design by Eliot Scott
Conceptual design by Brian Froud
Director of Photography: Alex Thomson, B.S.C.
Score composed by Trevor Jones
Songs composed and performed by David Bowie
Special Effects Supervisor: George Gibbs
Costume design by Brian Froud and Ellis Flyte

Featuring: David Bowie, Jennifer Connelly, Toby Froud

Howard the Duck (Released August 1, 1986)

A Lucasfilm Ltd. Production
A Universal Pictures release
Executive produced by George Lucas

Produced by Gloria Katz
Directed by Willard Huyck
Screenplay by Willard Huyck and Gloria Katz, based on the Marvel Comics
    character created by Steve Gerber
Edited by Michael Chandler and Sidney Wolinsky
Director of Photography: Richard H. Kline, A.S.C.
Production design by Peter Jamison
Music by John Barry
Sound design by Randy Thom
Visual Effects Supervisor: Michael J. McAlister
Costume Designer: Joe Thompkins

Featuring: Lea Thompson, Jeffrey Jones, Tim Robbins, Ed Gale, Chip Zien

Captain EO (Released at Disneyland September 13, 1986)

A George Lucas Presentation
Executive produced by George Lucas
Produced by Rusty Lemorande
Directed by Francis Coppola
Screenplay by George Lucas
Art direction by Geoffrey Kirkland
Cinematography Consultant: Vittorio Storaro
Choreography by Jeffrey Hornaday
Music by Michael Jackson
Theater and Costume Consultant: John Napier

Featuring: Michael Jackson, Anjelica Huston

Willow (Released May 20, 1988)

A Lucasfilm Ltd. Production in association with Imagine Entertainment
A MGM-UA release
Executive produced by George Lucas
Produced by Nigel Wooll
Directed by Ron Howard
Screenplay by Bob Dolman, from a story by George Lucas
Edited by Daniel Hanley and Michael Hill
Production design by Allan Cameron
Director of Photography: Adrian Biddle, B.S.C.
Music by James Horner
Sound design by Ben Burtt
Visual effects by Industrial Light & Magic (Dennis Muren, Michael J. McAlister,
    Phil Tippett)
Costume design by Barbara Lane

Featuring: Val Kilmer, Warwick Davis, Joanne Whalley, Jean Marsh, Patricia
    Hayes, Billy Barty, Pat Roach, Gavan O'Herlihy
Academy Award nominations: best sound-effects editing, best visual effects

Tucker: The Man and His Dream (Released August 12, 1988)

A Lucasfilm Ltd./Zoetrope Studios Production
A Paramount Pictures release
Executive produced by George Lucas

Produced by Fred Roos and Fred Fuchs
Directed by Francis Coppola
Screenplay by Arnold Schulman and David Seidler
Edited by Priscilla Nedd
Production design by Dean Tavoularis
Cinematography by Vittorio Storaro (AIC)
Music by Joe Jackson
Sound design by Richard Beggs
Costume design by Milena Canonero

Featuring: Jeff Bridges, Martin Landau, Joan Allen, Frederic Forrest, Mako,
    Dean Stockwell
Academy Award nominations: best art direction and set decoration, best cos-
    tume design, best supporting actor (Martin Landau)

Indiana Jones and the Last Crusade (Released May 24, 1989)

A Lucasfilm Ltd. Production
A Paramount Pictures release
Executive produced by George Lucas and Frank Marshall
Produced by Robert Watts
Directed by Steven Spielberg
Screenplay by Jeffrey Boam, from a story by George Lucas and
    Menno Meyjes
Edited by Michael Kahn, A.C.E.
Production design by Eliot Scott
Director of Photography: Douglas Slocombe
Music by John Williams
Sound design by Ben Burtt
Visual Effects Supervisor: Michael J. McAlister
Costume design by Anthony Powell

Featuring: Harrison Ford, Sean Connery, Denholm Elliott, Alison Doody, John
    Rhys-Davies, Julian Glover
Academy Award: best sound-effects editing
Academy Award nominations: best original score, best sound

Radioland Murders (Released October 21, 1994)

A Lucasfilm Ltd. Production
A Universal Pictures release
Executive produced by George Lucas
Produced by Rick McCallum and Fred Roos
Directed by Mel Smith
Story by George Lucas
Screenplay by Willard Huyck & Gloria Katz and Jeff Reno & Ron Osborn
Edited by Paul Trejo
Production design by Gavin Bocquet
Director of Photography: David Tattersall
Music by Joel McNeely
Costume design by Peggy Farrell

Featuring: Mary Stuart Masterson, Brian Benben, Ned Beatty, George Burns,
    Scott Michael Campbell, Brion James, Michael Lerner, Michael McKean,
    Jeffrey Tambor, Stephen Tobolowsky, Christopher Lloyd

TELEVISION FILMS

The Ewok Adventure: Caravan of Courage
(Initial broadcast on ABC November 25, 1984)

A Lucasfilm Ltd. and Korty Films Production
Executive produced by George Lucas
Produced by Thomas G. Smith
Directed by John Korty
Screenplay by Bob Carrau, from a story by George Lucas
Edited by John Nutt
Production design by Joe Johnston
Director of Photography: John Korty
Music by Peter Bernstein
Sound design by Randy Thom
Visual Effects Supervisor: Michael Pangrazio
Costume design by Cathleen Edwards and Michael Becker

Featuring: Eric Walker, Warwick Davis, Fionnula Flanagan, Aubree Miller
Emmy Award: outstanding special visual effects
Emmy Award nomination: outstanding children's programming (1984–85)

Ewoks and Droids Adventure Hour
(Ewoks and Droids: The Adventure of R2-D2 and C-3PO Animation, first-season initial broadcast on ABC September 7, 1985)

A Nelvana Production in association with Lucasfilm Ltd.
Executive produced by Miki Herman
Supervising Editor: Rob Kirkpatrick
Music by Taj Mahal (Ewoks) and Stewart Copeland (Droids)

Featuring the voices of Jim Henshaw and Cree Summer Francks (Ewoks), and Anthony Daniels (Droids)

Ewoks II: The Battle for Endor
(Initial broadcast on ABC November 24, 1985)

A Lucasfilm Ltd. Production
Executive produced by George Lucas
Produced by Thomas G. Smith
Written and directed by Jim and Ken Wheat, based on a story by George Lucas
Edited by Eric Jenkins
Production design by Joe Johnston and Harley Jessup
Director of Photography: Isidore Mankofsky, A.S.C.
Music by Peter Bernstein
Sound design by Randy Thom
Visual Effects Supervisor: Michael J. McAlister
Costume Supervisor: Michael Becker

Featuring: Wilford Brimley, Aubree Miller, Warwick Davis, Sian Phillips
Emmy Award: outstanding special visual effects
Emmy Award nominations: outstanding children's programming, outstanding sound mixing for a miniseries or special (1985–86)

The Great Heep
(Initial broadcast on ABC June 7, 1986)

A Nelvana Production for Lucasfilm Ltd. based on characters created by George Lucas
Executive produced by Miki Herman
Directed by Clive Smith
Screenplay by Ben Burtt
Production design by Joe Johnston
Music by Patricia Cullen and Patrick Gleeson, with songs by Stewart Copeland and Derek Holt
Sound design by Ben Burtt

Featuring: Anthony Daniels as C-3PO, Long John Baldry, Winston Rekert, Graeme Campbell

Ewoks
(Ewoks Animation second-season initial broadcast on ABC November 1, 1986)

A Lucasfilm Ltd. Production in association with Nelvana
Executive produced by Cliff Ruby and Elana Lesser
Story Editor: Paul Dini
Production design by Kirk Henderson
Music by Patrick Gleeson

Featuring the voices of James Cranna, Sue Murphy, Denny Delk, Jeanne Reynolds

Maniac Mansion
(Initial broadcast on the Family Channel September 14, 1990)

Produced by Atlantis Films Ltd. in association with the Family Channel and YTV/Canada, Inc. and Lucasfilm Ltd. Television
Based on the original computer game by Lucasfilm Games
Executive produced by Peter Sussman, Eugene Levy, and Barry Jossen
Series created by Michael Short, Eugene Levy, David Flaherty, and John Hemphill
Developed for television by Cliff Ruby, Elana Lesser, and Bob Carrau
Production design by Stephen Roleff
Director of Photography: Ray Braunstein
Music by Louis Natale

Featuring: Joe Flaherty, Deb Faker, Cathleen Robertson, George Buza, Mary Charlotte Wilcox, John Hemphill

The Young Indiana Jones Chronicles
(Initial broadcast on ABC March 4, 1992)

A Lucasfilm Ltd. Production
Executive produced by George Lucas
Produced by Rick McCallum
Directed by Bille August, Mike Newell, Nicolas Roeg, Terry Jones, David Hare, Gavin Millar, Carl Schultz, Simon Wincer, Deepa Mehta, Vic Armstrong, Michael Schultz, Peter MacDonald, Ben Burtt, Joe Johnston, Robert Young, Rene Manzor, Gillies MacKinnon, Dick Maas, Jim O'Brien, and Syd Macartney
Screenplays by Frank Darabont, Jonathan Hales, Matthew Jacobs, Carrie Fisher, Ben Burtt, Reg Gadney, Gavin Scott, Jonathan Hensleigh,

Rosemary Anne Sisson, and Jule Selbo, from a story by George Lucas
Edited by Ben Burtt, Janus Billeskov-Jansen, Edgar Burcksen, Louise
Rubacky, Paul Martin Smith, Tom Christopher, and Joan E. Chapman
Production design by Gavin Bocquet and Ricky Eyres
Director of Photography: David Tattersall, Jorgen Persson, Giles Nuttgens,
Oliver Stapleton, Miguel Icaza Solana, David Higgs, and Ashley Rowe
Music by Laurence Rosenthal, Joel McNeely, Steve Bramson, Curt Sobel, and
Frederic Talgorn
Costume design by Charlotte Holdich and Trisha Biggar

Featuring: Sean Patrick Flanery, Corey Carrier, Margaret Tyzack, Lloyd Owen,
Ruth DeSosa, Ronny Coutteure, George Hall
11 Emmy Awards
26 Emmy Award nominations
Banff Award: best continuing series
Golden Globe Award nomination
Angel Award: best drama series

VIDEO FILMS

THE YOUNG INDIANA JONES CHRONICLES

My First Adventure (Egypt, Tangiers, 1908)

A Lucasfilm Ltd. Production
Executive produced by George Lucas
Produced by Rick McCallum
Directed by Jim O'Brien and Michael Schultz
Screenplay by Jonathan Hales and Jule Selbo, based on a story by
George Lucas
Edited by Edgar Burcksen and Paul Martin Smith G.B.F.E.
Production design by Gavin Bocquet and Ricky Eyres
Directors of Photography: David Tattersall and Ashley Rowe
Music by Laurence Rosenthal
Supervising Sound Editors: Tom Bellfort and Larry Oatfield
Visual Effects Supervisors: Allison Smith-Murphy and Kristine Hanna
Costume design by Charlotte Holdich and Louise Page

Featuring: Corey Carrier, Margaret Tyzack, Ruth DeSosa, Lloyd Owen, Kevin
McNally, Rowena Cooper, Ashley Walters

Passion for Life (British East Africa, Paris, 1909)

A Lucasfilm Ltd. Production
Executive produced by George Lucas
Produced by Rick McCallum
Directed by Carl Schultz and Rene Manzor
Screenplay by Matthew Jacobs and Reg Gadney, based on a story by George Lucas
Edited by Edgar Burcksen
Production design by Gavin Bocquet
Directors of Photography: Miguel Icasa Solana and David Tattersall
Music by Laurence Rosenthal and Joel McNeely
Supervising Sound Editor: Tom Bellfort

Visual Effects Supervisor: Allison Smith-Murphy
Costume design by Charlotte Holdich

Featuring: Corey Carrier, Margaret Tyzack, Ruth DeSosa, Lloyd Owen, Danny
Webb, Jean-Pierre Aumont, Isaac Senteu Supeyo, James Gammon, Paul
Freeman, Lukas Haas

The Perils of Cupid (Vienna, Florence, 1909)

A Lucasfilm Ltd. Production
Executive produced by George Lucas
Produced by Rick McCallum
Directed by Bille August and Mike Newell
Screenplay by Matthew Jacobs and Jule Selbo, based on a story by George Lucas
Edited by Edgar Burcksen and Louise Rubacky
Production design by Gavin Bocquet
Directors of Photography: Jorgen Persson and David Tattersall
Music by Laurence Rosenthal
Supervising Sound Editor: Tom Bellfort
Visual Effects Supervisor: Allison Smith-Murphy
Costume design by Charlotte Holdich

Featuring: Corey Carrier, Margaret Tyzack, Ruth DeSosa, Lloyd Owen, George
Corraface, Lennart Hjulstrom, Ernst Hugo Jardegard, Bjorn Granat, Amalie
Alstrup, Max von Sydow

Travels with Father (Russia, Athens, 1910)

A Lucasfilm Ltd. Production
Executive produced by George Lucas
Produced by Rick McCallum
Directed by Michael Schultz and Deepa Mehta
Screenplay by Frank Darabont, Matthew Jacobs, Jonathan Hales, based on a
story by George Lucas
Edited by Paul Martin Smith G.B.F.E.
Production design by Ricky Eyres
Director of Photography: Giles Nuttgens
Music by Laurence Rosenthal
Supervising Sound Editor: Larry Oatfield
Visual Effects Supervisor: Susan Davis
Costume design by Trisha Biggar

Featuring: Corey Carrier, Lloyd Owen, Ruth DeSosa, Margaret Tyzack,
Michael Gough

Journey of Radiance (Banaras, China, 1910)

A Lucasfilm Ltd. Production
Executive produced by George Lucas
Produced by Rick McCallum
Directed by Deepa Mehta and Gavin Millar
Screenplay by Jonathan Hensleigh and Rosemary Anne Sisson, based on a
story by George Lucas
Edited by Louise Rubacky and Edgar Burcksen

Production design by Gavin Bocquet and Lucy Richardson
Directors of Photography: Giles Nuttgens and Oliver Stapleton
Music by Laurence Rosenthal
Supervising Sound Editor: Tom Bellfort
Visual Effects Supervisor: Allison Smith-Murphy
Costume design by Charlotte Holdich

Featuring: Corey Carrier, Margaret Tyzack, Ruth DeSosa, Lloyd Owen, John
    Wood, Dorothy Tutin, Ping Wu, Nigel Fan, Hemanth Rao

Spring Break Adventure (Princeton, Mexico, 1916)

A Lucasfilm Ltd. Production
Executive produced by George Lucas
Produced by Rick McCallum
Directed by Joe Johnston and Carl Schultz
Screenplay by Matthew Jacobs and Jonathan Hales, based on a story by
    George Lucas
Edited by Louise Rubacky, Edgar Burcksen, Paul Martin Smith G.B.F.E.
Production design by Gavin Bocquet, Ricky Eyres, Barbara Kretschmer, Jeffrey Ginn
Director of Photography: David Tattersall
Music by Laurence Rosenthal
Supervising Sound Editor: Tom Bellfort
Visual Effects Supervisors: Allison Smith-Murphy and Kristine Hanna
Costume design by Charlotte Holdich, Louise Page, Peggy Farrell

Featuring: Sean Patrick Flanery, Lloyd Owen, Ronny Coutteure, Robyn Lively,
    Francesco Quinn, Mike Moroff, Mark L. Taylor, Clark Gregg, James Handy

Love's Sweet Song (Ireland, London, 1916)

A Lucasfilm Ltd. Production
Executive produced by George Lucas
Produced by Rick McCallum
Directed by Gillies MacKinnon and Carl Schultz
Screenplay by Jonathan Hales and Rosemary Anne Sisson, based on a story
    by George Lucas
Edited by Edgar Burcksen and Louise Rubacky
Production design by Gavin Bocquet
Director of Photography: David Tattersall
Music by Laurence Rosenthal and Joel McNeely
Supervising Sound Editor: Tom Bellfort
Visual Effects Supervisor: Allison Smith-Murphy
Costume design by Charlotte Holdich

Featuring: Sean Patrick Flanery, Ronny Coutteure, Elizabeth Hurley, John
    Lynch, Shane Connaughton, Darragh Kelly, Susannah Doyle, Nell Murphy,
    Vanessa Redgrave, Kika Markham

Trenches of Hell (The Somme, Germany, 1916)

A Lucasfilm Ltd. Production
Executive produced by George Lucas
Produced by Rick McCallum
Directed by Simon Wincer

Screenplay by Jonathan Hensleigh, based on a story by George Lucas
Edited by Ben Burtt and Edgar Burcksen
Production design by Gavin Bocquet
Director of Photography: David Tattersall
Music by Frederic Talgorn
Supervising Sound Editor: Tom Bellfort
Visual Effects Supervisor: Allison Smith-Murphy
Costume design by Charlotte Holdich

Featuring: Sean Patrick Flanery, Ronny Coutteure, Jason Flemyng, Richard
    Ridings, Simon Hepworth, Jonathan Phillips, Yves Beneyton, Herve Pauchon

Demons of Deception (Verdun, Paris, 1916)

A Lucasfilm Ltd. Production
Executive produced by George Lucas
Produced by Rick McCallum
Directed by Rene Manzor and Nicolas Roeg
Screenplay by Jonathan Hensleigh and Carrie Fisher, based on a story by
    George Lucas
Edited by Ben Burtt and Louise Rubacky
Production design by Gavin Bocquet
Director of Photography: David Tattersall
Music by Joel McNeely
Supervising Sound Editor: Tom Bellfort
Visual Effects Supervisor: Allison Smith-Murphy
Costume design by Charlotte Holdich

Featuring: Sean Patrick Flanery, Ronny Coutteure, Domiziana Giordano,
    Kenneth Haigh, Ian McDiarmid, Jacqueline Pearce, Sheila Burrell, Maria
    Charles, Bernard Fresson, Jean Rougerie, Igor De Savitch, Cris Campion

Phantom Train of Doom (German East Africa, 1916)

A Lucasfilm Ltd. Production
Executive produced by George Lucas
Produced by Rick McCallum
Directed by Peter MacDonald
Screenplay by Frank Darabont, based on a story by George Lucas
Edited by Edgar Burcksen
Production design by Gavin Bocquet
Director of Photography: David Tattersall
Music by Joel McNeely
Supervising Sound Editor: Tom Bellfort
Visual Effects Supervisor: Allison Smith-Murphy
Costume design by Charlotte Holdich

Featuring: Sean Patrick Flanery, Ronny Coutteure, Lynsey Baxter, Tom Bell,
    Ronald Fraser, Paul Freeman, Freddie Jones, Norman Rodway

Oganga: The Giver and Taker of Life (German East Africa, Congo, 1916–17)

A Lucasfilm Ltd. Production
Executive produced by George Lucas
Produced by Rick McCallum

Directed by Simon Wincer
Screenplay by Frank Darabont, based on a story by George Lucas
Edited by Louise Rubacky
Production design by Gavin Bocquet
Director of Photography: David Tattersall
Music by Joel McNeely
Supervising Sound Editor: Tom Bellfort
Visual Effects Supervisor: Allison Smith-Murphy
Costume design by Charlotte Holdich

Featuring: Sean Patrick Flanery, Ronny Coutteure, Bryan Pringle, Michel Duchaussoy, Isaach De Bankole, Emile Abossolo M'Bo, Isolde Barth, Yann Colette, Friedrich Von Thun

Attack of the Hawkmen (Ravenelle, Ahlhorn, 1917)

A Lucasfilm Ltd. Production
Executive produced by George Lucas
Produced by Rick McCallum
Directed by Ben Burtt
Screenplay by Matthew Jacobs, Rosemary Anne Sisson, Ben Burtt, based on a story by George Lucas
Edited by Ben Burtt
Production design by Ricky Eyres
Director of Photography: Giles Nuttgens
Music by Joel McNeely
Supervising Sound Editor: Tom Bellfort
Visual Effects Supervisor: Susan Davis
Costume design by Trisha Biggar

Featuring: Sean Patrick Flanery, Ronny Coutteure, Patrick Toomey

Adventures in the Secret Service (Austria, Petrograd, 1917)

A Lucasfilm Ltd. Production
Executive produced by George Lucas
Produced by Rick McCallum
Directed by Vic Armstrong and Simon Wincer
Screenplay by Frank Darabont and Gavin Scott, based on a story by George Lucas
Edited by Edgar Burcksen and Louise Rubacky
Production design by Gavin Bocquet
Director of Photography: David Tattersall
Music by Laurence Rosenthal
Supervising Sound Editor: Tom Bellfort
Visual Effects Supervisor: Allison Smith-Murphy
Costume design by Charlotte Holdich

Featuring: Sean Patrick Flanery, Benedict Taylor, Matthew Wait, Christopher Lee, Patrick Ryecart, Jennifer Ehle, Jean-Pierre Cassel, Julia Stemberger, Gary Olsen, Beata Pozniak, Ravil Isyanov, Roger Sloman, Joss Ackland

Espionage Escapades (Barcelona, Prague, 1917)

A Lucasfilm Ltd. Production
Executive produced by George Lucas

Produced by Rick McCallum
Directed by Terry Jones and Robert Young
Screenplay by Gavin Scott, based on a story by George Lucas
Edited by Louise Rubacky and Joan E. Chapman
Production design by Gavin Bocquet
Director of Photography: David Tattersall
Music by Joel McNeely and Laurence Rosenthal
Supervising Sound Editor: Tom Bellfort
Visual Effects Supervisor: Allison Smith-Murphy
Costume design by Charlotte Holdich

Featuring: Sean Patrick Flanery, Tim McInnerny, Amanda Ooms, Timothy Spall, Kenneth Cranham, Harry Enfield, Terry Jones, William Hootkins, Liz Smith

Tales of Innocence (Northern Italy, Morocco, 1917)

A Lucasfilm Ltd. Production
Executive produced by George Lucas
Produced by Rick McCallum
Directed by Bille August and Michael Schultz
Screenplay by Jonathan Hales, based on a story by George Lucas
Edited by Janus Billeskov Jansen and Paul Martin Smith, G.B.F.E.
Production design by Gavin Bocquet and Ricky Eyres
Directors of Photography: Jorgen Persson and Ashley Rowe
Music by Laurence Rosenthal
Supervising Sound Editors: Tom Bellfort and Larry Oatfield
Visual Effects Supervisors: Allison Smith-Murphy and Kristine Hanna
Costume design by Charlotte Holdich and Louise Page

Featuring: Sean Patrick Flanery, Clare Higgins, Veronika Logan, Jay Underwood, Pernilla August

Daredevils of the Desert (Palestine, 1917)

A Lucasfilm Ltd. Production
Executive produced by George Lucas
Produced by Rick McCallum
Directed by Simon Wincer
Screenplay by Frank Darabont, based on a story by George Lucas
Edited by Ben Burtt
Production design by Gavin Bocquet
Director of Photography: David Tattersall
Music by Laurence Rosenthal
Supervising Sound Editors: Tom Bellfort and Larry Oatfield
Visual Effects Supervisors: Allison Smith-Murphy and Kristine Hanna
Costume design by Charlotte Holdich

Featuring: Sean Patrick Flanery, Catherine Zeta Jones, Julian Firth, Cameron Daddo, Douglas Henshall, Haluk Bilginer

Masks of Evil (Istanbul, Transylvania, 1918)

A Lucasfilm Ltd. Production
Executive produced by George Lucas
Produced by Rick McCallum

Directed by Mike Newell and Dick Maas
Screenplay by Rosemary Anne Sisson and Jonathan Hensleigh, based on a story by George Lucas
Edited by Louise Rubacky and Edgar Burcksen
Production design by Gavin Bocquet
Director of Photography: David Tattersall
Music by Laurence Rosenthal and Curt Sobel
Supervising Sound Editor: Tom Bellfort
Visual Effects Supervisor: Allison Smith-Murphy
Costume design by Charlotte Holdich

Featuring: Sean Patrick Flanery, Katherine Butler, Keith Szarabajka, Peter Firth, Bob Peck, Ahmet Levendoglu

Treasure of the Peacock's Eye (Egypt, Java, South Pacific, 1919)

A Lucasfilm Ltd. Production
Executive produced by George Lucas
Produced by Rick McCallum
Directed by Carl Schultz
Screenplay by Jule Selbo, based on a story by George Lucas
Edited by T. M. Christopher
Production design by Ricky Eyres
Director of Photography: David Tattersall
Music by Steven Bramson
Supervising Sound Editor: Tom Bellfort
Visual Effects Supervisor: Susan Davis
Costume design by Trisha Biggar

Featuring: Sean Patrick Flanery, Ronny Coutteure, Adrian Edmondson, Jayne Ashbourne, Tom Courtenay

Winds of Change (Paris, Princeton, 1919)

A Lucasfilm Ltd. Production
Executive produced by George Lucas
Produced by Rick McCallum
Directed by David Hare and Michael Schultz
Screenplay by Jonathan Hales, based on a story by George Lucas
Edited by Louise Rubacky and Paul Martin Smith, G.B.F.E.
Production design by Gavin Bocquet and Ricky Eyres
Directors of Photography: Giles Nuttgens and David Tattersall
Music by Joel McNeely and Laurence Rosenthal
Supervising Sound Editors: Tom Bellfort and Larry Oatfield
Visual Effects Supervisor: Allison Smith-Murphy
Costume design by Trisha Biggar and Charlotte Holdich

Featuring: Sean Patrick Flanery, Lloyd Owen, Cyril Cusack, Anna Massey, Michael Maloney, Douglas Henshall, Alec Mapa, Michael Kitchen, Josef Sommer, Jeroen Krabbe, Brooke Langton, Kevin Jackson, Stephen Michael Ayres

Mystery of the Blues (Chicago, 1920)

A Lucasfilm Ltd. Production
Executive produced by George Lucas

Produced by Rick McCallum
Directed by Carl Schultz
Screenplay by Jule Selbo, based on a story by George Lucas
Edited by Edgar Burcksen
Production design by Barbara Kretschmer
Director of Photography: David Tattersall
Music by Joel McNeely
Supervising Sound Editor: Tom Bellfort
Visual Effects Supervisor: Allison Smith-Murphy
Costume design by Peggy Farrell

Featuring: Sean Patrick Flanery, Harrison Ford, Jeffrey Wright, Jay Underwood, Keith David, Frank Vincent, Frederick Weller, Maria Howell, Nicholas Turturro, Saginaw Grant, Jane Krakowski, David Arnott, Victor Slezak, Ray Serra

Scandal of 1920 (New York, 1920)

A Lucasfilm Ltd. Production
Executive produced by George Lucas
Produced by Rick McCallum
Directed by Syd Macartney
Screenplay by Jonathan Hales, based on a story by George Lucas
Edited by Louise Rubacky
Production design by Jeff Ginn and Barbara Kretschmer
Director of Photography: David Tattersall
Music by Joel McNeely
Supervising Sound Editor: Tom Bellfort
Visual Effects Supervisor: Allison Smith-Murphy
Costume design by Peggy Farrell

Featuring: Sean Patrick Flanery, Alexandra Powers, Anne Heche, Jennifer Stevens, Jeffrey Wright, Christopher John Fields, Tom Beckett, Michelle Nicastro, Bill McKinney, Robert Trebor, Peter Appel, Annabelle Gurwitch, Mark Holton, Terumi Matthews, Dylan Price, Joshua Rifkind, Peter Spears, Brenda Strong, Guri Weinberg

Hollywood Follies (Hollywood, Newhall, 1920)

A Lucasfilm Ltd. Production
Executive produced by George Lucas
Produced by Rick McCallum
Directed by Michael Schultz
Screenplay by Jonathan Hales and Matthew Jacobs, based on a story by George Lucas
Edited by Paul Martin Smith, G.B.F.E.
Production design by Ricky Eyres
Director of Photography: Ross Berryman A.S.C.
Music by Laurence Rosenthal
Supervising Sound Editor: Larry Oatfield
Visual Effects Supervisor: Susan Davis
Costume design by Peggy Farrell

Featuring: Sean Patrick Flanery, Allison Smith, Bill Cusack, Julia Campbell, David Margulies, Peter Dennis, Tom Beckett, Luigi Amodeo, J. D. Hinton, Leo Gordon, Stephen Caffrey, Dana Gladstone

GEORGE LUCAS CREDITS ON NON-LUCASFILM PRODUCTIONS

Kagemusha (The Shadow Warrior) (Released October 1980)
A 20th Century-Fox release. A film by Akira Kurosawa. Executive producers of the international version: George Lucas and Francis Coppola

Body Heat (Released August 1981)
A Warner Brothers release. A Ladd Company Presentation. Written and directed by Lawrence Kasdan. Executive producer (uncredited): George Lucas

Return to Oz (Released June 1985)
A Buena Vista release. Directed and cowritten by Walter Murch. Credit at end: "Special Thanks to Robert Watts and George Lucas"

Powaqqatsi (Released April 1988)
A Cannon Group release. A Francis Ford Coppola and George Lucas Presentation. A film by Godfrey Reggio

The Land Before Time (Released November 18, 1988)
A Universal Pictures release. A Don Bluth production. Executive producers: Steven Spielberg and George Lucas. Script by Stu Krieger, from a story by Judy Freudberg and Tony Geiss. An animated feature

INDUSTRIAL LIGHT & MAGIC FILM CREDITS

1977
Star Wars (20th Century-Fox/Lucasfilm Ltd.)
   Academy Award: best visual effects

1980
The Empire Strikes Back (20th Century-Fox/Lucasfilm Ltd.)
   Academy Award: best visual effects

1981
Dragonslayer (Paramount)
   Academy Award nomination: best visual effects
Raiders of the Lost Ark (Paramount/Lucasfilm Ltd.)
   Academy Award: best visual effects

1982
The Dark Crystal (Henson Productions)
E.T. The Extra-Terrestrial (Universal)
   Academy Award: best visual effects
Poltergeist (MGM/UA)
   Academy Award nomination: best visual effects
   British Academy Award: best visual effects
Star Trek II: The Wrath of Khan (Paramount)
Twice Upon a Time (Korty/Lucasfilm Ltd.)

1983
Return of the Jedi (20th Century-Fox/Lucasfilm Ltd.)
   Academy Award: best visual effects
   British Academy Award: best visual effects

1984
The Ewok Adventure (20th Century-Fox Television/Lucasfilm Ltd.)
   Emmy Award: best visual effects
Indiana Jones and the Temple of Doom (Paramount/Lucasfilm Ltd.)
   Academy Award: best visual effects
   British Academy Award: best visual effects
The Neverending Story (Bavaria Studios)
Starman (Columbia)
Star Trek III: The Search for Spock (Paramount)

1985
Amazing Stories (Universal Television/Amblin)
Back to the Future (Universal/Amblin)
   British Academy Award nomination: best visual effects
Cocoon (20th Century-Fox)
   Academy Award: best visual effects
Enemy Mine (20th Century-Fox)
Ewoks: The Battle for Endor (20th Century-Fox Television/Lucasfilm Ltd.)
   Emmy Award: best visual effects
Explorers (Paramount)
The Goonies (Warner Bros./Amblin)
Mishima (Warner Bros.)
Out of Africa (Universal)
Young Sherlock Holmes (Paramount/Amblin)
   Academy Award nomination: best visual effects

1986
Captain EO (Disney) 3-D Film for Disneyland
General Cinema Trailer (General Cinema Corp.)
The Golden Child (Paramount)
Howard the Duck (Universal/Lucasfilm Ltd.)
Labyrinth (TriStar/Hanson Prod.)
The Money Pit (Universal/Amblin)
Star Trek IV: The Voyage Home (Paramount)

1987
Batteries Not Included (Universal/Amblin)
   Academy Award: technical achievement
Empire of the Sun (Warner Bros./Amblin)
Harry and the Hendersons (Universal/Amblin)
Innerspace (Warner Bros./Amblin)
   Academy Award: best visual effects
Star Tours (Disney/Lucasfilm Ltd.) Simulator Ride for Disneyland
Star Trek: The Next Generation (Paramount Television) "Journey to Farpoint"
The Witches of Eastwick (Warner Bros.)
   British Academy Award: best visual effects

1988
Caddyshack II (Warner Bros.)
Cocoon: The Return (20th Century-Fox)
Star Trek Attraction (Universal/Paramount) Universal Studios Tour
Who Framed Roger Rabbit (Touchstone Pictures/Amblin)

Academy Award: best visual effects
British Academy Award: best visual effects
Willow (MGM/UA/Lucasfilm Ltd.)
Academy Award nomination: best visual effects

1989

The Abyss (GJP Productions/20th Century-Fox)
Academy Award: best visual effects
Always (Amblin/Universal)
Back to the Future, Part II (Amblin/Universal)
Academy Award nomination: best visual effects
British Academy Award: best visual effects
Body Wars (Disney) Simulator Ride for Walt Disney World's EPCOT Center
The 'Burbs (Renfield Productions/Universal)
Field of Dreams (Universal)
Ghostbusters II (Columbia)
Indiana Jones and the Last Crusade (Lucasfilm Ltd./Paramount)
Mickey-Eisner Spot (Disney)
Skin Deep (Blake Edwards Co.)
Tummy Trouble (Disney)

1990

Akira Kurosawa's Dreams (Kurosawa Productions/Warner Bros.)
Back to the Future, Part III (Amblin/Universal)
Die Hard 2 (20th Century-Fox)
Ghost (Paramount)
The Godfather, Part III (Paramount)
The Hunt for Red October (Paramount)
Joe Versus the Volcano (Warner Bros.)
Roller Coaster Rabbit (Disney)

1991

Backdraft (Imagine Films)
Academy Award nomination: best visual effects
The Doors (TriStar)
Hook (Columbia/Amblin)
Academy Award nomination: best visual effects
Hudson Hawk (TriStar)
Mickey's Audition (Disney)
The Rocketeer (Disney)
Space Race (Showscan) Simulator Ride
Star Trek VI (Paramount)
Academy Award nomination: best visual effects
Switch (HBO Films)
Terminator 2: Judgment Day (Carolco/TriStar)
Academy Award: best visual effects
British Academy Award: best visual effects

1992

Alien Encounter (Showscan) Simulator Ride
Alive (Disney/Paramount)
Death Becomes Her (Universal)
Academy Award: best visual effects
British Academy Award: best visual effects
Memoirs of an Invisible Man (Warner Bros.)
The Young Indiana Jones Chronicles (Lucasfilm Ltd.)

1993

Fire in the Sky (Paramount)
Jurassic Park (Amblin/Universal)
Academy Award: best visual effects
British Academy Award: best visual effects
Last Action Hero (Columbia Pictures)
Manhattan Murder Mystery (TriStar)
Meteorman (MGM/UA)
The Nutcracker (Warner Bros.)
Rising Sun (20th Century-Fox)
Schindler's List (Amblin/Universal)

1994

Baby's Day Out (Columbia)
Disclosure (Warner Bros.)
The Flintstones (Amblin/Universal)
Forrest Gump (Paramount)
Academy Award: best visual effects
British Academy Award: best visual effects
The Hudsucker Proxy (Warner Bros.)
The Mask (New Line Cinema)
Academy Award nomination: best visual effects
British Academy Award nomination: best visual effects
Maverick (Warner Bros.)
Radioland Murders (Lucasfilm Ltd./Universal)
Star Trek Generations (Paramount)
Wolf (Columbia)

1995

The American President (Columbia/Castle Rock)
Casper (Amblin/Universal)
Congo (Paramount)
The Indian in the Cupboard (Paramount)
In the Mouth of Madness (Katja/New Line Cinema)
Jumanji (TriStar)
Sabrina (Paramount)
Village of the Damned (Universal)

1996

101 Dalmatians (Disney)
Daylight (Universal)
Dragonheart (Universal)
Eraser (Warner Bros.)
Mars Attacks! (Warner Bros.)
Mission: Impossible (Paramount)
Special Effects (An IMAX Film) (WGBH)
Star Trek: First Contact (Paramount)
Twister (Warner Bros./Universal)

1997

The Absent Minded Professor (Disney)
The Lost World: Jurassic Park (Amblin/Universal)
Men in Black (Columbia)
Spawn (New Line Cinema)
Speed 2 (20th Century-Fox)
Star Wars Trilogy Special Edition (20th Century-Fox/Lucasfilm Ltd.)

INDUSTRIAL LIGHT & MAGIC
A SELECTION OF COMMERCIAL CREDITS

1992
British Petroleum "Elevator" (W. B. Doner)

1993
Acura "Hot Wheels" (Ketchum)
ESPN "Speedworld" (ESPN)

1994
AT&T "River" (McCann Erickson)
Energizer "Darth Vader" (Chiat/Day)
Oldsmobile Aurora "Painting," "Assembly" (Leo Burnett)

1995
BMW "Penguin" (Fallon McElligott)
Coke "Convoy" (W. B. Doner)
Ford "This is Escort" "Reflections" (J. Walter Thompson)
New World Telephone "Launch" (Bozell)
Pepsi "Casper-Stuck" (BBDO)
Supercuts "Stylin" (J. Walter Thompson)

1996
AT&T "Kabuki" (BBDO)
Citroën "Saxo" (EURO RSCG SCHER LAFARGE)
Compuserve "Whale" (Martin Williams)
Dodge "Hang Ten" (BBDO)
General Motors EV1 "Appliances" (Hal Riney & Partners)
Honda "Newspaper" (Rubin Postaer and Associates)
Intel "Carpet" (Dahlin Smith White)
Nissan "Pigeons" (TWBA Chiat/Day)
Snapple "Mikey" (Kirshenbaum Bond & Partners)
Snickers "Elephant Walk" (BBDO)

SKYWALKER SOUND FILM CREDITS

1977
Star Wars (20th Century-Fox/Lucasfilm Ltd.)
   *Special Achievement Academy Award for Special Sound and Voice
      Creation: Ben Burtt (Sound Designer)
   *Note: A.M.P.A.S. did not give an award for sound-effects editing until 1981

1980
The Empire Strikes Back (20th Century-Fox/Lucasfilm Ltd.)
   Academy Award: best sound

1981
Raiders of the Lost Ark (Paramount/Lucasfilm Ltd.)
   Academy Award: best sound-effects editing

1982
E.T. The Extra-Terrestrial (Universal)
   Academy Awards: best sound, best sound-effects editing

1983
Koyaanisquatsi (Cannon)
Return of the Jedi (20th Century-Fox/Lucasfilm Ltd.)
   Academy Award nomination: best sound

1984
The Ewok Adventure: Caravan of Courage (20th Century-Fox Television/
   Lucasfilm Ltd.)
Indiana Jones and the Temple of Doom (Paramount/Lucasfilm Ltd.)
Trilogy: The Making of a Saga (Lucasfilm Ltd.)

1985
Cocoon (20th Century-Fox)
The Dream Is Alive (IMAX)
Ewoks II: The Battle for Endor (20th Century-Fox Television/Lucasfilm Ltd.)
Explorers (Paramount)
Fletch (Universal)
The Grand Canyon (IMAX/Cinema Group)
Latino (Cinecom)
The Legend of Billie Jean (TriStar)
The Mean Season (Orion)
Mishima (Warner Bros.)
Wild Rose (New Front/Ely Lake)

1986
Captain EO (Disney) 3-D Film for Disneyland
Howard the Duck (Universal/Lucasfilm Ltd.)
Remo Williams: The Adventure (Orion)

1987
Alamo (IMAX/Texas Cavalcade)
Gardens of Stone (TriStar)
Niagara (IMAX/Texas Cavalcade)
Spaceballs (MGM/UA)
Star Tours (Disney/Lucasfilm Ltd.) Simulator ride for Disneyland

1988
Cocoon: The Return (20th Century-Fox)
Colors (Orion)
The Couch Trip (Orion)
The Land Before Time (Universal)
Powaqqatsi (Cannon)
Tucker: The Man and His Dream (Paramount/Lucasfilm Ltd./Zoetrope)
Willow (MGM/UA/Lucasfilm Ltd.)
   Academy Award nomination: best sound-effects editing

1989
Always (Amblin/Universal)
Body Wars (Disney) Simulator ride for Walt Disney World's EPCOT Center
Cold Dog Soup (Handmade Prods.)
Driving Miss Daisy (Warner Bros.)
Fletch Lives (Universal)

Indiana Jones and the Last Crusade (Lucasfilm Ltd./Paramount)
    Academy Award nomination: best sound
    Academy Award: best sound-effects editing
Romero (Four Seasons)

1990
Avalon (TriStar)
The Godfather, Part III (Paramount)
Henry & June (Universal)
The Hot Spot (Orion)
Wild at Heart (PolyGram)

1991
Backdraft (Imagine Films)
    Academy Award nominations: best sound, best sound-effects editing
Bugsy (TriStar)
The Five Heartbeats (20th Century-Fox)
F/X II (Orion)
Rush (MGM/UA)
Soapdish (Paramount)
Space Race (Showscan)
Terminator 2: Judgment Day (Carolco/TriStar)
    Academy Awards: best sound, best sound-effects editing

1992
Polynesian Odyssey (IMAX)
A River Runs Through It (Columbia)
Single White Female (Gramercy)
To Be An Astronaut (IWERKS)
Toys (20th Century-Fox)
The Young Indiana Jones Chronicles (Lucasfilm Ltd.)
    Emmy Award: best sound

1993
Jurassic Park (Amblin/Universal)
    Academy Awards: best sound, best sound-effects editing
Meteorman (MGM/UA)
Mrs. Doubtfire (20th Century-Fox)
The Nutcracker (Warner Bros.)
Rising Sun (20th Century-Fox)
The Saint of Fort Washington (Warner Bros.)

1994
Baby's Day Out (Columbia)
Disclosure (Warner Bros.)
Forrest Gump (Paramount)
    Academy Award nominations: best sound, best sound-effects
        editing
Grand Canyon (IMAX/Cinema Group)
Honey, I Shrunk the Audience (Disney)
The Journey Inside (IMAX/Intel Corp.)
Miracle on 34th Street (20th Century-Fox)
Quiz Show (Buena Vista)
Radioland Murders (Lucasfilm Ltd./Universal)
Return of the Jedi (Foreign Video) (20th Century-Fox/Lucasfilm Ltd.)
Yellowstone (IMAX/Destination Cinema)

1995
Casper (Amblin/Universal)
Celluloid Closet (Sony Classics)
Circle of Life (Disney)
The Great American West (IMAX/Utah Productions)
Home for the Holidays (20th Century-Fox)
The Hunted (Universal)
Jumanji (TriStar)
Nine Months (20th Century-Fox)
Ozarks (IMAX/ITEC Attractions)
Picture Bride (Miramax)
Species (MGM/UA)
Strange Days (20th Century-Fox)
Toy Story (Disney)
Zion (IMAX/Kieth Merrill Productions)

1996
The Arrival (Orion)
Ellen's Energy Crisis (Walt Disney Theme Park Prod./EPCOT)
Enchanted Castle (IWERKS/Destination Cinema)
The Great White Hype (20th Century-Fox)
James & The Giant Peach (Disney)
Mars Attacks! (Warner Bros.)
Mexico (IMAX/Sol Film)
Mission: Impossible (Paramount)
One Fine Day (20th Century-Fox)
Special Effects (IMAX/WGBH)

1997
Beverly Hills Ninja (Sony Pictures/MPCA)
The Lost World: Jurassic Park (Amblin/Universal)
Mimic (Miramax)
Out to Sea (20th Century-Fox)
Reach the Rock (Universal)
Star Wars Trilogy Special Edition (20th Century-Fox/Lucasfilm Ltd.)
Volcano (20th Century-Fox)

LUCASARTS ENTERTAINMENT COMPANY GAME CREDITS (DOMESTIC PLATFORMS)

1982–86
Ballblazer, Koronis Rift, Labyrinth, PHM Pegasus, Rescue on Fractalus, and
    Strike Fleet (Developed for publication by other companies)

1987
Maniac Mansion (IBM, Amiga, Atari ST, C-64, Apple II)

1988
Battlehawks 1942 (IBM, Amiga, Atari ST)
Zak McKracken (IBM, Amiga, Atari ST, C-64, Apple II)

1989

Indiana Jones and the Last Crusade: The Graphic Adventure (IBM, Amiga,
  Atari ST, Macintosh)
Pipe Dream (IBM, Amiga, Atari ST, Macintosh)
Their Finest Hour: The Battle of Britain (IBM, Amiga, Atari ST)

1990

Loom (IBM, Amiga, Atari ST, Macintosh)
Night Shift (IBM, Amiga, Atari ST, Macintosh)
The Secret of Monkey Island (IBM, Amiga, Atari ST, Macintosh)

1991

Monkey Island 2: Lechuck's Revenge (IBM, Amiga, Color Macintosh)
Secret Weapons of the Luftwaffe (IBM)
Star Wars (NES)
SWOTL Tours (P-80, P-38, Hel62, Do335) (IBM)

1992

Classic Adventures (IBM)
Defenders of Dynatron City (NES)
The Empire Strikes Back (NES)
Indiana Jones and the Fate of Atlantis (IBM, Amiga, Color Macintosh)
Loom (PC CD-ROM)
The Secret of Monkey Island (PC CD-ROM)
Super Star Wars (SNES)
SWOTL/4 SWOTL Tours (PC CD-ROM)

1993

Air Combat Classics (IBM)
Day of the Tentacle (IBM, PC CD-ROM, Color Macintosh)
Indiana Jones and the Fate of Atlantis (PC CD-ROM)
Rebel Assault (PC CD-ROM, Sega CD)
Sam & Max Hit the Road (IBM)
Super Empire Strikes Back (SNES)
X-Wing, Imperial Pursuit, B-Wing (IBM)
Zombies Ate My Neighbors (SNES)

1994

Rebel Assault (Macintosh CD)
Sam & Max Hit the Road (PC CD-ROM)
Star Wars Screen Entertainment (Windows, Macintosh)
Super Return of the Jedi (SNES)
Tie Fighter, Defender of the Empire (IBM)
X-Wing Collector's CD (PC CD-ROM)

1995

Dark Forces (PC CD-ROM, Macintosh CD)
The Dig (PC CD-ROM)
Full Throttle (PC CD-ROM, Macintosh CD)
The LucasArts Archives Vol. I (PC CD-ROM)
Rebel Assault II: The Hidden Empire (PC CD-ROM, Macintosh CD)
Tie Fighter Collector's CD-ROM (PC CD-ROM)

1996

Afterlife (Windows 95/DOS/Macintosh CD)
Dark Forces (PlayStation)

The Dig (Macintosh CD)
Indiana Jones and His Desktop Adventures (Windows, Macintosh)
The LucasArts Archives Vol. II: The Star Wars Collection (IBM)
LucasArts Macintosh Archives Vol. I (Macintosh CD)
Mortimer and the Riddles of the Medallion (Windows 95, Macintosh CD)
Rebel Assault II: The Hidden Empire (PlayStation)
Shadows of the Empire (Nintendo 64)

1997

Ballblazer Champions (PlayStation)
Curse of Monkey Island (Windows 95 CD)
Herc's Adventures (Saturn, PlayStation)
Jedi Knights: Dark Forces II (Windows 95, Macintosh CD)
The LucasArts Archives Vol. II: The Star Wars Collection (Macintosh)
Outlaws (Windows 95, Macintosh CD)
Star Wars Rebellion (Windows 95 CD)
Tie Fighter Collector's CD-ROM (Macintosh CD)
X-Wing vs. Tie Fighter (PC CD-ROM)
Yoda Stories (Windows 95 CD)

Note: The following credits for the *Star Wars Trilogy Special Edition* became
available after this book went to press.

Star Wars Special Edition (Released January 31, 1997)
Special Edition Producer: Rick McCallum
Special Edition Editor: T. M. Christopher
Visual Effects Supervisors: Alex Seiden, John Knoll, Dave Carson, Stephen
  Williams, Dennis Muren, Joseph Letteri, and Bruce Nicholson
Visual Effects Producers: Tom Kennedy and Ned Gorman

The Empire Strikes Back Special Edition (Released February 21, 1997)
Special Edition Producer: Rick McCallum
Special Edition Editor: T. M. Christopher
Visual Effects Supervisor: Dave Carson
Visual Effects Producer: Tom Kennedy

Return of the Jedi Special Edition (Released March 14, 1997)
Special Edition Producer: Rick McCallum
Special Edition Editor: T. M. Christopher
Music by John Williams
Jedi Rocks music by Jerry Hey
Visual Effects Supervisors: Dave Carson and John Knoll
Visual Effects Producer: Tom Kennedy

INDEX

PHOTOGRAPH CREDITS

Unless noted below, all photographs in this book are © Lucasfilm Ltd. Numbers refer to pages.